The 'Say Walahi' Generation

Identity, Profiling, & Survival in Canada

A Somali Canadian Perspective

Ahmed Ali Ilmi

Nsemia

First Edition: April 2013

Published by: Nsemia Inc. Publishers (www.nsemia.com)
Oakville, Ontario, Canada

Cover illustration by:
Cover Design by: Danielle Pitt
Book Layout Design: Kemunto Matunda

Note for Librarians:

A cataloguing record for this book is available from Library and Archives Canada.

ISBN: 978-1-926906-28-7

DEDICATION

For my parents Ali Ilmi Warsama, Amina Ahmed Hure, and the
Ilmi Family

TABLE OF CONTENTS

ACKNOWLEDGEMENTS

Bims Allah, ar-Rahman ar-Rahim – In the name of God, Most Gracious, Most Merciful. I wish to thank, first and foremost, Allah for all of his blessings.

I wish to thank my beloved parents, Aabo and Hoyooo, and the entire Ilmi family for all their love and support. Their prayers and guidance have pushed me to go the distance. They have sacrificed tremendously for me to take this journey. I will be forever indebted to all of you.

I acknowledge Njoki Wane who has had the most profound impact on my scholarship and personal development as a Somali. Your courses have moved my soul and allowed me for the first time in my academic life to speak about being Somali. This journey couldn't have been possible without you constant support and your believing in me. Professor Wane your support as an African elder, teacher, mentor, friend, and scholar has inspired me to be the scholar that I am today. I am so grateful to your facilitation of a learning environment in which I could theorize my embodied Indigenous knowledge and lived experiences. Thank you for all your support, confidence, and willingness to push me throughout this journey.

Professor George Dei, your scholarship and activisms have truly inspired me to decolonize my spirit. Thank you.

Professor Paul Olson, your friendship and academic mentorship has been delightful and though provoking. Thank you for your scholarship and laying down the foundation for this book.

I wish to acknowledge Fouzia Warsame who I have had some of the most profound conversations throughout this journey and who has struggled almost as I did to complete this journey. Your constant feedback and mentorship have allowed me to dig deep in my soul to reflect on some of my most personnel experiences. Fouzia your support as sister, friend, and a fellow Somali scholar has pushed further than I could go in academia. You have enabled me to own this journey and to cherish the writing process. Your unwavering believe in my passion have propelled me to heights that I never imaged. Thank you for taking this journey with me. I will forever be in debited to you.

I wish to acknowledge my best friend Abdijalil Wardhere and his family for helping me through all the way and for believing in me. You have served me as a cultural mentor and I constantly sought your advice and moral support through writing this book.

I wish to thank Hamza Abdullahi, for his friendship and dedication to this project. The friendship that we have developed throughout this project is something that I will forever treasure.

Finally, I would like to thank the Somali community in the GTA. The community has raised me well and inspired me to go the distance.

ABSTRACT

The aim of the study is to look at the social formative processes of the Somali-Canadian youth, known as the *'Say-walahi'* generation. My research will primarily focus on how I learned to survive as a racialized person in the White Canadian nation space while holding onto my Somali identity, and how my journey diverges and converges with Somali-Canadian youth. First, I examine how the media socially constructed the Somali identity through a colonial gaze in a *Toronto Life* article. Secondly, I narrate some of my own schooling experiences for they speak to the deep psychological and spiritual scars that I embody as a racialized Somali. Especially, my interest is to show how instrumental Somali *dhaqan* was to my survival under the colonial/ racializing gaze. Finally, I stress the importance of and the need for Somali youth to engage in de-colonizing/ de-racialization processes that encompasses their re-discovery of their Indigenous Somali-ness.

ABOUT THE AUTHOR

Ahmed Ali Ilmi is a PhD candidate in the Department of Sociology and Equity Studies at the Ontario Institute for Studies in Education of the University of Toronto. His research interests are in the areas of Indigenous Knowledges, Anti-Racism Studies, Anticolonial Thought, Diasporaic Indegenity, and the History of Social Movements in Somalia.

Chapter One

My Journey, Their Journey, Our Journey

Introduction

The Somali Community is amongst one of the newest communities to arrive in Canada, which began growing in the 1990s, and is also the largest racialized/Black community in the GTA. As an African immigrant population, they are socially, politically, and economically excluded from ever becoming full citizens of this land, similar to previous generations of African-Canadians that have been racialized. According to Galabuzi (2006), the process of racialization "involves the construction of racial categories as real, but also unequal, for the purposes that impact the economic, social, and political composition of a society...Racialization translates into actions and decisions within a system that lead to differential and unequal outcomes, and the entrenchment of structures of oppression" (p. 34). Somali-Canadian youths, commonly referred to as 'Say-Walahi' by older generation Somalis, are suffering from marginalisation and social exclusion because they are marked as racialized by mainstream Canadian society. The term 'Say-Walahi' is a fusion of English and Somali, which loosely translates to 'swear to God'; this term signifies the youth's hybrid existence in which they straddle two worlds. This age group is the first generation of ethnic Somalis to be raised in Canada and are often faced with the challenges of having to negotiate their identities in the Canadian social environment that has systematically racialized them (Ibrahim, 2008). This revelation has stressed the necessity for me as a Somali–Canadian to look at our common experiences; my journey of cultural resistance, their necessary journey of culture re-discovery and our collective journey of survival. The timing of my research is crucial to our survival, to bridge the gap between younger and older generation Somalis through the telling of my story. Somali-Canadian youth are being deprived of achieving any meaningful success in their lives as a result of their racialized status. In addition, the 'Say-Walahi' generation is the largest voiceless segment of our Canadian society. As such, there are no existing avenues in which Somali-Canadian youth can express themselves.

I believe that by engaging in the politics of cultural resistances, that I can assist Somali-Canadian youth to recognise and resist all the ways in which misrepresentation has framed them. I further believe that by engaging in the cultural struggle, as a powerful tool of de-colonization/ de-racialization, Somali-Canadian youth will be able to regain their humanity, as this process will allow them to see themselves outside the Eurocentric discourse and imagery that is recognised as their identity. The process of cultural resistance and cultural rediscovery will allow Somali youth to collect themselves from the margins, regroup, and collectively stand together in the path of change. In addition, it will allow them to break free from their imposed 'Somali-ness,' which are formed from the violent images in the civil war regime, discourse, and historization that is produced by Western societies. Graveline (1998) reminds us that "for every act of authority...is resistance...in some form embodied...enacted. Our lived experience... How we resist is culture... is context bound as is how we exert authority" (33). At present, the *'Say-Walahi'* youth are socialised through their culture and in their homes to be Somali and African, while they are simultaneously marked as racialized Black youths by the greater Canadian society. The act of revisiting the past and embracing the histories of the Somali identity, both in pre-colonial times and after the tragic partition of Africa, (which Somali youth embody) is essential to any wholesome cultural/self-recovery processes; the past is within us and it informs our identity.

The purpose of my research is to provide an opposing view to the negative discourse about Somalis. My research will primarily focus on how I learned to overcome these generalisations by holding onto my Somali identity, culture and language and how my journey differs and intersects with Somali-Canadian youth of today. Moreover, by looking at my own Somali social formation process, by committing myself to identity recovery, and by engaging in self-de-colonization/de-racialization as a form of resistance, I will show how instrumental Somali *dhaqan* [ancestral way of life] was in my own identity struggles as a Somali youth.

Personal Location

As a first generation Somali-Canadian, my research requires that I articulate multiple, complex identity issues that I faced as a part of the first wave of Somali immigrant children to have been educated in Canadian schools in the early 1990s. In adjusting to my new home away from home, I witnessed my Somali identity getting trapped and tied to the civil war regime that has displaced millions of Somalis across the globe. Although I was fortunate enough to have physically escaped the civil war in my homeland, the psychological trauma was inescapable because the darkest moments in the history of the Somali peoples have been captured by Western media. As a teenager, the mid-1990s were especially difficult, as this coincided with the high point of the civil war, with a growing anti-Somali sentiment in the GTA and with the discovery that my life as a Somali youth was negatively impacted by presumptions that abound labelling Somalis as nomadic, welfare bums, violent and uncivilized. In this formidable time, my body became a text to be read by both Somalis and non-Somalis: To the Somali community I was a lost Westernized teen, but to mainstream society I was a "Black youth" who required constant surveillance for the greater good of the Canadian society. In this fragmented subsistence, I began to submerge myself in a process of 'cultural production' that allowed me to embrace my *dhaqan* [Somali ancestral way of life] within the Canadian context as a form of resistance and survival. This process served as a survival mechanism, allowing me to regain my humanity as well as to recapture my Indigenous Somali identity, despite the debilitating effects of both a community in crisis and the racialization of mainstream society.

Admittedly, my reclaiming journey has not been an easy one. I was constantly subjected to Western social formative processes that sought to amputate and marginalise my Somali-ness as a new immigrant in Canada. My cultural ways were considered inferior, and my mother tongue was foreign and therefore forbidden in school, even when I was addressing other Somali students. I remember being told that I had to speak English in order to increase my chances of "making it" in Canada. Each day I was forced to leave my Somali identity at home; this foreign existence was a constant frustration which eventually led to my displacement, exile and subsequent dislocation.

For instance, on multicultural days, my primary and high school parties were merely a facade, a superficial acknowledgment that other cultures existed. It was my hope that I would be given an opportunity to display and express my Somali culture. Unfortunately, the opportunity brought much disappointment. My cultural foods were never appreciated by the teacher and other students whenever I brought them to school. This experience was the beginning of many traumatic episodes. It was at this moment that I realised that

I needed to fervently hold on to my cultural ways of knowing in order to survive. Whether I chose to assimilate or maintain my Somali identity, I was not accepted in this Canadian context; this realisation was a hard adjustment for me. For the first few years in the Canadian school system, I was unable to distinguish which days were school days and which were holidays because weekends in Somalia were on Thursdays and Fridays. My unfamiliarity was inadvertently conveyed to my first homeroom teacher, when I announced "*see you tomorrow*" on a Friday, thinking that Saturday was a school day.

Unfortunately, I learned to exist in relative silence, wherein my identity has always been subject to being read through a colonial lens. Similar to Malidoma Somé (1995), I had to subsist within two contradictory world views. I learned to interact and understand the dominant Eurocentric social environment, while simultaneously maintaining my ability to see the world from a Somali cultural vantage point that has kept me grounded in my Indigenous ways of knowing. This dichotomous existence has caused me much frustration, and left me feeling disconnected from my own community. In addition, I always felt like that community did not understand how difficult it was for me to function as a "Somali" caught between two worlds. Nothing around me reflected positive images of Somali culture, except in my home environment. Conversely, everything that I did, in the Somali community's eyes, was perceived as somewhat mysterious, and at times dysfunctional because of my ability to adopt the Western way of dress and language, which was different from our Somali culture. The precarious space that I occupy, my lived experience, my passion and my commitment to dislodge the Somali identity from the crux of civil war, required that I begin the process of identity recovery, de-colonization and de-racialization, which is the thrust behind my research.

Organization of this Book

In this book, I will have six chapters. Chapter one, my introduction, provides an overview of my work. Chapter two, my discursive frameworks, indicate theories I utilise to analyse the complex identity issues facing the Somali community, in particular, Somali-Canadian youth, and conceptualises critical moments in my social formation. Chapter three provides an analysis of a 1995 article in *Toronto Life* magazine titled, "**Dispatch from Dixon**", which describes the

Somali as having a primitive, Third-World identity. Chapter four, my journey through schooling in the Canadian landscape, tells the story of my encounter with colonial education. Chapter five, Somali youth cultural disconnect, examines the issues of Somali youth's cultural dislocation and consequent identity fragmentation. Chapter six, my conclusion, is a reflection on the Somali community's journey, and my journey, and offers Somali *dhaqan* as an avenue for the '*Say-Walahi*' to resist colonization/racialization.

Chapter One introduces the Somali-Canadian youth, referred to as the '*Say-Walahi*' generation, and gives a brief synopsis of some of the issues that they are going through as a result of their racialized status in the White Canadian Nation State. It will also examine the complex identity crisis that the '*Say-Walahi*' generation often find themselves in as a result of the two identities that they embody (Somali and Canadian). I also locate myself in this chapter, and revisited some of my own identity struggles as a way to make use of my own story to stress the importance of de-colonizing/de-racialization of the Somali identity. Theoretical frameworks to be employed and the precise reasoning for utilising every method will be stated in this chapter as well.

Chapter Two indicates the discursive frameworks that I make use of in this work. This research utilises an anti-colonial framework to clarify and theorise the social construction of the Somali national character. In addition, my anti-racist discursive framework examines the colonial reasoning for which the Somali community was racialized. In order to bring a Somali voice to the centre of my research, I utilise my own narrative to reflect on my own stories of survival and cultural re-discovery. I also draw on some of the Somali community's narratives that offer Somali *dhaqan* as resistance against colonization, to show how the Somali community dealt with and continues to deal with colonization/racialization from a Somali vantage point.

Chapter Three examines how the media has depicted Somalis as uncivilized, undeserving, and problematic members of a tribal community as in the case of a *Toronto Life* article, *"Dispatch from Dixon"*— written in the summer of 1995, during the height of the influx of Somali's into Canada. My analysis will examine three interviews in the above article to indicate how the Somali identity was socially constructed through a colonial gaze. Particular attention will be given to how the authors of such articles and publications use racial discourse and colonial ideology as a means to dehumanize the Somali national character in the White Canadian nation space. I will conclude this chapter with a self-reflective analysis indicating how I felt after reading this article and how I subsequently decided to respond to it. This chapter speaks of our journey in the White Canadian nation space.

Chapter Four focuses on my experiences within the Canadian educational system. As such, I tell some of my untold stories of being racialized as a Somali youth in the Ontario school system. I will explain the social processes which were ascribed to my psyche during my formative years. I will also indicate how Somali *dhaqan* offered me an Indigenous holistic perspective from which I was able draw on my embodied knowledge to escape the constant colonial gaze in school. My narrative will also challenge the prevailing violent images, stereotypes, and dehumanizing discourses that abound with respect to Somalia and Somali people. By revisiting issues that have wrought havoc on my spirit, I hope to bring closure to negative memories of my schooling past and enter into a place of healing from which I can envision a brighter future for the *'Say-Walahi'* generation. In essence, this chapter speaks to my journey in the White Canadian nation space.

Chapter Five delves into the importance of and the need for Somali youth to engage in de-colonizing/de-racialization processes that encompasses their re-discovery of their Somali-ness and their embodied rich histories. The notion of developing and engaging in identity re-claiming as a wholesome way of negotiating one's self will be indicated. I will study issues of the 'Say-Walahi' generation's cultural disconnect: issues of Somali-youth identity fragmentation, which resulted from being physically, psychologically, and culturally disjointed from their homeland, are also studied in this chapter. As a case study, I will analyse a conference video of the first annual Ohio Youth Summit to compare presentations made by two Somalis, to show the intergenerational cultural gaps that exist between elders and Somali youth. Ultimately, this chapter offers Somali dhaqan, as the only way of liberating oneself and recovering one's voice. The power of speaking with a single Somali communal voice as a way of resisting fragmentation and supporting the collection of the Somali identity is also amplified in this chapter. With notions of voice, language will be taken up as a mechanism of creating a sheltered safety zone and exercising self-determination.

Chapter Six concludes with reflecting on the themes that were presented and the narratives that were collected. Also, future directives for research on the *'Say-Walahi'* generation will be discussed. I will also take a moment to breathe and think about the lessons that I have learned from undertaking this research. As I conclude, I am aware that I am not undertaking this project merely to advance my academic career. This journey has been riddled with many questions of what has pushed me to write this piece of work. My resolve and firm belief is that there is a greater purpose and something within me that has driven and will continue to drive me to realise the outcome of this project goes beyond academic walls and extends into the Somali community. The necessity of Somali youth to undertake a cultural re-discovery/re-claiming journey is articulated in this chapter.

Chapter 2

Discursive Framework

I have chosen to utilise an anti-colonial and anti-racist conversational framework, coupled with an autobiographical narrative to facilitate an in-depth textual analysis of the complex identity issues facing the Somali community, and in particular, the *'Say-Walahi'* generation. The anti-colonial framework offers a possible historical understanding of the social construction of the Somalis as colonized peoples. It also allows us to understand the complex colonial ideologies that are used to socially construct the Somalis as a 'Third-World,' primitive, and undeserving community. Anti-colonial discursive frameworks allow me to understand how a 'refugee crisis' was constructed in the media to marginalise the Somalis as the community was settling in Canada. Hall (1981) explains racist ideology as being a practice that "has its own specific settings (sites) - especially in the apparatus of ideological production which produce social meanings and distribute them throughout society, like the media" (p. 12). In agreement with Hall's ideas, this theory will enable me to interrogate the media's racist beliefs. Also this framework will enable me to understand the language and discourses employed by the media to legitimise racism during the height of influx of Somali immigrants into Canada.

Anti-colonialism is centred on taking up the struggle of any colonized peoples and reclaiming their identities after a colonial encounter. Dei (1999) in *Indigenous Knowledges in a Global Context* conceptualises anti-colonial discursive framework as a discourse that

> emphasizes the power held by local/social practice to survive the colonial and colonized encounters. It argues that power and discourse are not processed solely by the 'colonizer'. Discursive agency and power of resistance reside in and among colonized and marginalized groups...Anti-colonial theorizing arises out of alternative, oppositional paradigms, which are in turn based on Indigenous concepts and analytical systems and cultural frames of reference. (p. 7)

Notions of re-discovering Indigenous identities, complete with cultural knowledge and wholesome existence, speak to the concept of re-claiming the Somali identity from the margins, as a way of picking up the pieces and moving beyond fragmentation. Identity encompasses elements of 'knowledge production' and Indigenous cultural capital that is vital to the social wellbeing of the community, in particular the *'Say-Walahi'* generation. This theory is useful in allowing me to look back at how the Somali community dealt with racial discrimination in the early 1990s and how the Somali community continues to deal with racialization. Anti-colonial frameworks will enable me to theorise the Somali community's narratives and interpret them from a critical lens to bring forth my understanding of Somali voices. Additionally, anti-colonialism is important to Somalia's communal voice recovery as a key aspect of de-colonizing/de-racialization the young minds of Somali-Canadian youth by stressing the importance of narratives and reflective analysis as a way of expressing collective healing and coming to terms with the brutalities of colonization. In essence, anti-colonial thought "is the emergence of a new political, culture, and intellectual movement reflecting the values and aspirations of colonized and resisting peoples/subjects" (Dei and Kempf, 2006, p. 4). As such, this framework permits me to place my cultural ways of knowing at the centre of my scholarship and enables me to interpret my world from a Somali perspective.

The discourse of anti-colonialism will guide my quest for liberation from the colonial domination I experienced in the Canadian education system. Although I am not located in the colonial education of my native land [Somalia], in Canada, education was used to socially dominate and control my mind. As such, my cultural knowledges were always devalued in the school system. Wane (2006) asserts "this has been done through a system of education, text, and literature. [Education] not only facilitated [colonization], but actively left deep spiritual and mental scars, causing mental and physical enslavement."(p. 88). As a mechanism of resistance, the anti-colonialism perspective infuses Indigenous ways of knowing to counter colonial aggression and contest cultural domination in schools.

Anti-colonial frameworks provide multiple views of the de-humanizing social formative processes the *'Say-Walahi'* generation undergo. Moreover, anti-colonial theory can be used to examine complex identity dislocation which concerns Somali youth in every aspect of their lives. I believe that one of the most detrimental aspects of the Somali societal struggle is internalisation and the acceptance of the dominant belief that places "tribalism" at the centre of Somalia's civil conflict, this paints Somalia as a "failed dysfunctional state" without any account for colonialism, and its role in the "current state of affairs" in Somalia. Accordingly, Wane (2006) points out that the processes of colonization involved "re-writing history to denying their existence, devaluating their knowledge, and debasing their cultural beliefs and practices" (87). Understanding this process is vital for any voice-recovery to occur, as Somali youth look at their histories, culture, and tradition outside the Eurocentric social construction. Anti-colonial discourse will provide me a lens with which to visualize my own identity outside the colonial histories that I embody and make sense of my Somali-ness in the White Canadian nation space. To grasp the social implication of the processes by which Somalis were/ are racialized, it is imperative for me to use anti-racism discourse in conjunction with anti-colonial framework.

An anti-racism framework compliments anti-colonialism by deconstructing the social processes of racialization and assists in making sense of how racism continues to devastate the community. According to Hall (1981) "Racism has a long, distinguished history in [Western] culture. It is grounded in the relations of slavery, colonial conquest, economic exploitation and imperialism, in which European races have stood in relation to the 'native people' of the colonized and exploited periphery" (p. 14). In working with Hall's (1981) conceptualisation of racism, an anti-racist framework enables me to place race at the centre of my research. I will employ this theory to interrogate and expose the root causes of the 'Somali refugee' crisis in Canada. This theory will also assist me in identifying the role the media played in producing such a crisis in the minds of the Canadian public. This framework enables me to also contextualise questions of power relations to reveal how dominant groups mark Somalis as the 'Other'. In addition, I can highlight how racially loaded language was used to dehumanize Somalis while presenting the community as troublesome to mask issues of racism in Canada. According to Dei (1996), the anti-racism paradigm is

> an action-oriented strategy for institutional, systemic change to address racism and interlocking systems of social oppression. Anti-racism is a critical discourse of race and racism in society and of the continuing racializing of social groups for differential and unequal treatment. Anti-racism

explicitly names the issues of race and social difference as an issue of power and equity...The historical processes of European colonization, culture and political imperialism, and enslavement of the world's Indigenous and non-White people are juxtaposed to simplistic notions of racial domination and difference based on skin color and "natural" difference. (p. 25)

In agreement with Dei's (1996) contention, this theory enables me to explain how racism is not highlighted as being the root cause of the injustices that were/are inflicted on the Somali community. Anti-racism framework is a sophisticated educational tool one can employ to challenge the status quo and question how the dominant groups maintain a social, political, and economical hierarchy. As such, "[the] impetus for anti-racism change comes from local communities' political struggles which challenge the Canadian state to live up to the true meanings of democratic citizenship, social justice, equity, and fairness"(Dei,1996, 25). As a result, this framework will allow me to examine institutional racism, notably within the implications of how the 'immigration debate' has been articulated in the media. The issues that face the Somali community as they settle in Canada are very complex and demand closer examination of how systemic racism has been instrumental in marginalising the Somali community. Hennery and Tatar (2006) explain systemic racism as referring to the

laws, rules, and norms woven into the social system that result in an unequal distribution of economic, political, and social resources and rewards among various racial groups... systemic racism is manifested in the media by, for example, the negative representation of people of colour, the erasure of their voices and experiences, and the repetition of racist images and discourse. (p. 55)

Concurring with Hennery and Tatar's (2006) theories, this framework will enable me to interrogate systemic inequities that have marginalised the Somali community.

My lived experiences and social location as a first generation Somali-Canadian necessitates my need to describe the numerous, multifaceted identity issues that I faced in the school system within the discourse of anti-racism. The theoretical framework of anti-racism speaks to my fragmented identity and to the unhealed wounds that I carry, and it accounts for the oppression that has been inflicted upon me as a member of a minority group (Dei, 1999). Moreover, the anti-racism framework is a sophisticated tool that I can use to deconstruct the social processes of racialization and to make sense of the grim realities that I was exposed to in the education system. As well, anti-racism encompasses principles that will allow me to closely examine White (male) power and privilege, and to question their dominance (Dei, 1996). Anti-racism discourse and education is not concerned merely with intellectualizing race, it also encompasses political action and community building (ibid.). This leaves room for me as a researcher to push the debate on questions revolving around race. Anti-racism also addresses the marginalisation of minority voices and the devaluation of their knowledge and lived experience. It encourages oppressed peoples to speak in their own voices (Dei, 1999). Thus, it permits me to situate myself in my research as a Somali and then examine how schooling played a part in marking me a dysfunctional "Black body." The anti-racism framework is also confrontational; it challenges the dominant discourse of Canadian multiculturalism (Dei, 1999). Henceforth, with this model I will critique the myth of Canada as the land of opportunity for all by examining how my identity was racialized as I entered the White Canadian nation space.

This framework has tools with which I can critically re-examine my educational past as well as understand how this colonial education system has shaped me and continues to dislocate my African-centric roots. In addition, this framework will provide me with the tools to (a) tell my untold stories of surviving the Eurocentric schools system in Ontario, (b) broach my Somali *dhaqan* as a means of resistance to colonization/racialization, and (c) highlight the significance of African-centric schools as the vanguard of the holistic African-Canadian communal existence. Theoretically, anti-racism provides room for one to speak about their lived experiences in their own voice. Therefore, it is essential for me to utilise a narrative framework to tell my own story in my own voice.

By utilising my narrative as a theoretical framework, it will be grounded in my Somali-ness, which gives me an opportunity to speak about my journey from an Indigenous perspective. It accredits my identity struggles, and theorises critical moments in my social formative life. I have chosen to use this theory to draw on some of my untold stories in a Somali voice, not to gain sympathy from the readers, but rather, to inject elements of Somali *dhaqan* in this research. My narrative is a de-colonizing/de-racializing tool that speaks to my desire to converse with a more holistic self. My narrative also affirms my right to be in an academic arena as a Somali-Canadian despite being marked as a 'dysfunctional Black youth' in the Ontario high school education system. I never thought a day would come in which I could speak about my 'schooling experiences' as a racialized body. As such, my long awaited story speaks to the endless possibilities of a decolonized Indigenous mind. Now that the opportunity has arrived after many years of sacrifice and endurance, it is imperative that I not only hold up the mirror to gaze at my unhealed wounds, but rather, that I truly deviate from the Eurocentric ways of knowing to embrace Indigenous Somali *dhaqan.*

As a Somali, this framework also allows me to indicate how I shall use my Indigenous background to resist colonization/racialization. This work has led me to a self-discovery process and has awakened my consciousness of a Somali communal existence that has enabled me to cope with being constantly marked as 'Other'. This research affirms my disconnected self from my physical existence as an Indigenous body that was "trying to make it" in mainstream society. As such, my Indigenous voice was always silenced by the dehumanizing Eurocentric images, and discourses that were ascribed to my identity. Consequently, I present a decolonized Somali self, as I strive with mind, body, and sprit to achieve and overcome the oppressive elements of my past. A narrative framework will enable me to centre myself in my research. Employing this example allows me to use Somali language to articulate feelings, thoughts, and communal collective knowledge that cannot be translated into English, the language of my formal education.

My Somali narrative is derived from my understanding of my communal histories, experiences, and *dhaqan* knowledges. Therefore, utilising storytelling will enable me to convey the Somali community's "collectively and communally shared [knowledges]" (Wane, 2008, p.191). I view Somali *dhaqan* as avenue of social action and collective resistance. Dei (1999) explains cultural knowledges as being

> Diverse and complex given the histories, cultures, and lived realities...While Indigenous knowledges are characterized

by the absence of colonial and imperial imposition, such knowledges emerge in the contemporary sense partly in response to colonial and 'postcolonial' intrusions. In other words, Indigenous knowledges are emerging again in the present day as a response to the growing awareness that the world's subordinated peoples and their values have been marginalized such that their past and present experiences have been flooded out by the rise in the influence of Western industrial capital. (p. 6)

In my efforts to speak about my community's journey, it is vital for me to bring a collective Somali voice to my work and to move beyond academic theorising. Re-telling some of the community's tales not only signifies the path that we have travelled together, but also speaks of the decolonizing strategies that we have collectively utilised to survive. It also stresses the necessity for future generations to take their own journeys to decolonize their minds, bodies, and souls. This framework will enable me to also offer Somali *dhaqan* as an avenue of resistance to all the ways in which Somali youth identities are built by mainstream society.

Chapter 3
Social Construction of the Somali Identity
in the White Canadian Nation State

Background

This chapter illustrates how the Somali community's identity was constructed through the colonial gaze of the Western media as we began to settle in Canada. . My aim is to show how the categorization of Somalis as 'Other' continues to marginalise the community. Clearly understanding this process is essential, because it has and continues to have profound implications on how Somalis are viewed today. The media's social construction of my Somali-ness signifies my journey and that of other Somali youth of becoming a racialized body in the Canadian landscape.

In this chapter, I reveal the Canadian media's construction of the Somali identity as uncivilized, undeserving, and problematic members of the wider Canadian society. As an example, I will analyse the 1995 article in Toronto Life magazine, **"Dispatch from Dixon"**—written by a freelance journalist named Daniel Stoffman during the height of the influx of Somalis into Canada. I will concentrate on three interview conversations. Particular attention will be given to how the author expresses racial discourse and colonial ideology as a means of dehumanizing the Somali national character in the White Canadian nation space. I will conclude this chapter with a self-reflective analysis of how I dealt with my spiritual injury after reading this article and how I am still processing the article.

Dixon is a north Etobicoke neighbourhood located in Toronto, Canada. The community of Dixon is made up of six high-rise condominium buildings on Dixon road. This neighbourhood is one of the first locations in which many of Toronto's early Somali arrivals have settled, including my family, in the late 1980s and early 1990s. At first, Dixon was a welcoming place in which many Somalis established a home away from home. I remember when we arrived at Pearson International Airport, my uncle pointed to the white buildings and said "sarahaas cadcad waa xaafad layiraah Dixon oo Soomalida badab koodu ku noolyihin" [See those tall white buildings? They are called Dixon and that is where all the Somalis live in Toronto]. Our first apartment was rented from Julius, a Venezuelan immigrant.

Although Dixon was not quite like home, we soon settled into our new life and I did not want to move out of this place, when my parents bought a house after a few years of living in this community. In Dixon, the Somali people formed a very tight-knit community. In addition, all the Somali cultural practices were followed. When people met in the hallways, elevators, etc., they greeted and treated each other with respect. Also, all the Somalis knew one another and if I ever got into trouble at the playground as a child, my parents would certainly find out.

Little did I know, this way of living would not last after my family and I moved from this community a year after arriving in Canada. Now Dixon inhabitants were socially shunned and were being referred to as a primitive, Third World, undeserving community by some in the Canadian media. In order to explain this change of perspective, I will provide the reader with three stories that the media carried that portrayed the Dixon community in derogatory terms. My reading of the newspaper articles' accounts of Dixon makes me wonder what the agenda was. In addition, I ask myself, did the community just sit and let the media paint these negative images? Did any community member voice their concerns? This book forms a part of my resistance and also serves as a counter narrative to those articles. I employ an anti-colonial lens to show that Somalis did not just sit; they resisted and they held on together and they maintained their cultural independence, thereby ensuring they did not lose their identity to the Canadian multicultural rhythm.

The article, "**Dispatch from Dixon**," opens by stating the number of people who live in the condominiums on Dixon Road. There is no doubt in the reader's mind that the place is crowded and that Somalis can be found everywhere. This article makes reference to a 1993 CBC film documentary, "**A Place Called Dixon**," that depicted the Somali community as a social hazard from a 'Third World primitive culture'. The author clearly paints the story quite vividly so that there is some resemblance between the article and the CBC documentary.

I will invite you as the reader to draw your own conclusions as you read below the stories of Mrs. Anab Osman[1], a woman who embodies Somali identity ; of Mr. Bob Swan a Canadian Baptist minister, who is introduced as someone who is friendly and supportive of the Somali community and has "help[ed] ethnic Somalis in Kenya; and of Mr. Nor, referred to as the 'Sheik' and the community elder by

---

1 Somali identity is the African ethnicity that was being marked as the "

the interviewer. The interviewer was Mr. Daniel Stoffman, a White journalist.

Dixon road is very close to the Toronto International airport and the sound of the planes arriving and leaving is so loud that the journalist starts his articles by describing this experience when he states, "A large incoming jet rattles the windows of Dahir Nor's apartment." Mr. Nor describes the north-Etobicoke neighbourhood, as 'the Promised Land' for Somalis in refugee camps. From what Mr Nor tells the journalist, Dixon is well known to the Somalis living abroad in refugee camps, even among those who cannot locate Canada on the world map.

As I went through the article, one particular statement stood out for me, "Nowhere could be more unlike Somalia, a tropical nation of nomadic camel herders, than this modern suburb. Yet some 4000 Somalis live in [Dixon]." It is clear from this statement that the journalist does not have much knowledge of Somalia because camels only live in the non-tropical areas of the country, and they are typically found in the harsher dry parts of the country. However, his reference to "a tropical nation of nomadic…" demonstrates the notion of Them vs. Us – the Non-Canadians vs. the Canadians. This description places the Somalis living in Dixon as outside the Canadian mainstream society.

What should one do to provide a counter argument to show that the journalist's views are biased and skewed? Where should I start to write my story to show that there is much more to us than being a people who have an address at Dixon? Where should I start to show that we do have a past and a rich history and that the journalist's writing perpetuates a particular discourse of marginalisation and production of colonial knowledge of 'Othering'? Is this journalist aware that he is participating in colonial knowledge production? The journalist's article is indicative of the colonial rhetoric on the Somali national character. It is left to the reader to formulate a particular kind of fictitious "Somali identity" hailing from the foreign land of Somalia with a very foreign lifestyle.

The author introduces Mrs. Anab Osman, as the first Somali he met and he says that she started talking to her about the Somali diaspora and how Somalis are "just like the Chinese and the Jews, the East Indians and the Hungarians, Somalis have spread across the globe". He also says that she has some twenty-five siblings, who are scattered across the world as a result of the civil war. With this brief introduction that Mr. Stoffman staged as being an interview about the Somali immigration experience, after one meeting with Anab Osman, the author, a White male, gets acquainted with the Somali people.

Mr. Bob Swan is introduced by the journalist, as someone who is friendly with Somalis and "understands their political and social structures." He then gives a short biography: Mr. Swan, a biologist who spent ten years working in Kenya with ethnic Somalis, has now moved into Dixon to "help Somalis resettle in Canada," as the author puts it. Mr. Swan is then quoted saying that he had first heard of Dixon in a refugee camp, where a Somali told Mr. Swan that his brother lives in Dixon. Mr. Swan did not know what Dixon was until the Somali man showed him an envelope with a return address that told him that it was an Etobicoke neighbourhood.

I am not sure whether Mr Nor was aware of how his interview would be used or how his words would be interpreted. Mr. Nor, who is referred by the journalist as a "talkative, sociable man who loves an audience," is never introduced properly. Mr. Stoffman also mentions that Mr. Nor holds a degree in Economics and speaks five languages and that he was recently laid off from a plastic factory job. Although the author states that Mr. Nor is an early Somali arrival to Dixon, he does not indicate how Mr. Nor qualified to immigrate to Canada, whether through the point system and/or if Mr. Nor was a refugee claimant. Yet, Mr. Nor's educational attainment and his language skills present him as an overqualified immigrant who had scored high in the point system. Of course, the credentials of Mr. Nor also make him more credible in the eyes of the Canadian general public. Yet, the journalist never questions why such an educated individual is working in a factory. Moreover, the author draws on cultural representation to qualify Mr. Nor's ability to represent the community. Consequently, he is also given the "Sheik" title to enhance his profile before the Canadian readers of this article. In Islamic culture, the title "Sheik" is only given to someone with religious stature in his community and this title is the equivalent of a priest in Christianity or rabbi in Judaism. To many non-Muslim Canadian readers who are unfamiliar with Somali Muslims, this title presented Mr. Nor as a religious figurehead worthy of speaking on behalf of his community. The writer of this article personifies Mr. Nor in such a way that allows Nor's credibility to maliciously batter the Somali community, as I will demonstrate later on in my analysis.

Colonizing the Somali Identity

I would like to turn my attention to Ann McClintock's (1995) work on gender and imperialism. McClintock's (1995) work examines how women served as the boundary markers of Empire. She suggests that colonial explorers routinely imagined their colonial encounters as being between themselves and native women and that woman often signified an ambiguous point of contact. Mr. Stoffman's interview with Mrs. Anab Osman can be equated as a colonial encounter, because he meets her first, and thus she signifies the Somali people. Then he proceeds with his colonial exploration by conducting the interview in such a way that subjects the Somali community. McClintock (1995) suggests that is typical colonial positioning in any encounter between the colonized and the colonizer, in which:

> European men crossing the dangerous thresholds of their known, they ritualistically feminized borders and boundaries. Female figures were planted at ambiguous points of contact ...women served as mediating and threshold figures by means of which men oriented themselves in space as agents of power and agents of knowledge. (p. 24)

Switching his interview style, the journalist now delves into the personal experiences of his subject and he begins by unfolding the events that touched Mrs. Anab Osman — her father was imprisoned "after running afoul" of the ruling regime in Somalia— to show how she was personally touched by tragedy. He also quotes Mrs. Anab Osman saying, "Everyone remembers all the terrible history, but now we have to build ways of dealing with the future" — hinting that she is looking forward to a brighter future in Canada and is not planning to go back to Somalia. The journalist deliberately uses quotes from Mrs. Anab Osman to begin articulating an anti-immigration discourse and to reclaim Canada's sovereignty from the invading Somalis, which is a figment of his colonial imagination. McClintock (1995) refers to a "visible trace of paranoia [ignited by] the male loss of boundary" (p.24). It is with this sense of panic that the author beings articulating anti-immigration/anti-Somali, racially loaded discourse to marginalise the Somali community. As such, Mr. Stoffman begins to carry out his counter response to the threat that is posed by Mrs. Anab's intent to stay permanently in Canada, which is again largely a figment of his imagination.

Then the author says that some refugees return to their homelands once the situation there improves and asks Mrs. Anab Osman if she would ever consider returning to Somalia. In response, she says, "I would never go back to live there." With his question and Mrs. Anab Osman's subsequent response, the author begins constructing a "refugee crisis" of illegitimate Somali refugees entering into Canada marked by the presence of Mrs. Anab Osman in the White Canadian nation space, as McClintock (1995) would argue. As such, the writer states that [Mrs. Anab Osman] had mentioned to him that she and her husband came to Canada as refugees from the United States and that her husband used to work for the Somali Embassy in the United States and that [her husband] used "to drive around Washington D.C. with a diplomatic flag on his car."

Under the 1951 United Nation Convention relating to the Status of Refugees, article 1, section B, states that any person(s) having a "well-founded fear of being persecuted for reasons of race, religion, nationality, membership of a particular social group or political opinion," (OHCR, 2009) qualifies as a refugee. Therefore, Mrs. Anab Osman and her husband as individuals who were living in the United States with diplomatic status do not qualify to be granted protection as refugees under international law. The writer at that moment goes on to raise some questions about "how close one had to be to the Siad Barre[2] regime, to work in the Somali Embassy in the United States and why someone residing in the US makes a refugee claim." He also says that "Somali gangs are not shooting civilians in the streets of Washington." With these statements, he raises serious questions that imply that Mrs. Anab Osman's refugee claim is a fraudulent one. At this critical juncture, the author insinuates the illegitimacy of the Somalis' status in Canada, with which Mrs. Anab Osman, portrayed as a primitive, passive, immigrant woman, naively appears to agree. Mr. Stoffman takes this opportunity to misrepresent the Somali culture and "orient [himself] in space as an agent of power and agent of knowledge" (McClintock, 1995, p. 25). Therefore, he is never to be questioned, and his views represent the establishment with full authority.

It is with this colonial frame of mind that the author carries out his colonial conquest through his article. Mrs. Anab Osman's alleged mention of her husband's Somali Embassy job creates a "colonial moment of discovery" (McClintock, 1995, p. 25), in which the writer, as a representative of Western civilization, can unveil the true motives of Somalis as they arrive in the "White Canadian nation space". This moment allows the author to embark on a colonial expedition that

2 Siad Barre was the President of Somalia from 1969 to 1991.

is marked by his journalistic violence to degrade the Somali national character in his article. This colonial mind-set also allows the author to be the sole interpreter of what he has found, as did previous European colonizers, in agreement with McClintock's (1995) ideas of the nature of colonial discoveries. Mr. Stoffman, through his act of "discovery," begins writing this article with a more aggressive colonial undertone, and he fragments the Somali identity to realise his colonial/anti-immigration agenda. Moreover, throughout this article he begins to map out his new found colonial territory (ibid.).

Colonial Actors at Work: Minister Bob Swan

I would like to utilise Chinua Achebe's (1996) classic novel *Things Fall Apart* to examine the role of missionaries in dismantling African societies. In Achebe's novel the author highlights the role of missionaries through a fictional character named Mr. Brown. In **"Dispatch from Dixon"** the role of the missionary is played by Bob Swan, a Canadian Baptist Minister. My aim is to illustrate how Minister Swan is instrumental in dehumanizing the Somali people by, first, bringing the refugee crisis to the author's attention; second, by painting Somalis as uncivilized, nomadic people who are living in the "Biblical age;" and thirdly, by dismissing the rights of Somali people to claim refugee status. I have chosen to draw on Achebe's (1996) work because it allows me to extrapolate Mr. Swan's deliberate articulation of racist, anti-Somali discourse. He presented himself as someone who was sympathetic to Somalis when we were becoming refugees across the globe. He then proceeded to hijack the collective voice of the Somali people when Somalia was falling apart by speaking against Somalis.

I would like to examine Mr. Swan's imperialistic politics and draw on them from a critical moment in the novel in which Okonkwo, the main character of Achebe's (1996) novel, invites his mother's kinsmen to his compound in Mbanta before he departs to his hometown of Umuofia. One of the Elders rises to his feet to thank Okonkwo and begins to talk about the importance of kinsmen, especially to the community's youth, and the significance of speaking in one's communal voice (Achebe, 1996).

As a Somali, the ability of my community to speak in one voice is a cultural pillar that Somalis have relied on for our subsistence for generations. It represents an existence in a community, a culture, and a way of life that is wholesome. Its collective meaning encompasses political, social, and cultural integrity. The ability to speak in one's voice for Somalis signifies our ability as a people to articulate and express ourselves. That is why I decided to connect the Elder's communal address, while the community is still intact and has not yet fallen to colonialism, to the moment that the Somali culture was fragmented in the *Toronto Life* article.

In addition to being a Baptist minister, Mr. Swan has worked with ethnic Somalis in Kenya. He is much like Mr. Brown, the friendly minister in Achebe's (1996) novel. Both ministers only see their relationship to the non-European peoples through a colonial lens. Mr. Brown directly represents his Queen in the novel and only sees his relationship with the people of Umuofia through an imperial lens, in which he only sees the locals as the subjects of her Majesty the Queen of England (Achebe, 1996). Mr. Swan, much like Mr. Brown, only sees Somalis through a historical colonial lens in which Somalis are still British subjects. This is represented in the way he uses the colonial works of Margaret Lawrence, a Canadian imperialist novelist who travelled to North Somalia in 1960 when it was called "Somaliland" and was under British colonial rule, to reproduce colonial ideology about his Somali subjects.

The author goes on to identify Somalis as primitive nomads, using Mr. Swan as the colonial expert who tries to bring his civilization into the Somali cultural landscape. But, before he does so, he describes Mr. Swan preparing dinner at his apartment, for a guest, who happens to be a refugee from Cameroon, who is watching a French TV channel, and says that he has to get to a basketball game that he runs at a local gym. The author indicates this to the readers to show that Mr. Swan is indeed carrying on humanitarian work to try to settle newcomers in Toronto. But, in reality Mr. Swan, like Mr. Brown in the novel, is getting acquainted with the subjects that he deemed to be an expert in (Achebe, 1996). As such, it is through the relationships that Mr. Brown develops with the locals, that he uses to undermine the community when the Queen's Royal District Commissioner decides to bring in his colonial administration (ibid). Much like the novel, it is through Mr. Swan's missionary lens, that the Somali community is seen as inferior and ultimately dehumanized.

Mr. Stoffman also uses Mr. Swan's so-called expertise to place Somalis in "biblical times." Mr. Swan begins marking his territorial colonial knowledge by tapping into Margaret Laurence's (1988) imperialist novel, *The Prophet's Camel Bell*, to describe Somalis as having an incredible ability to survive in the desert. What is even more disturbing for me as a Somali is that Mr. Swan points to a copy of Laurence's book as he begins to articulate his notions about Somalis. In essence, it is through this colonial text that Mr. Swan is reading Somalis, as pointed out by Wane (2006) when she wrote, "knowledge that appear(s) in texts are not neutral, because cultural activists are implicit in text. Texts are a result and embodiment of [colonial] processes and are by no means simple transmissions of facts" (p. 91). In fact, he directly reads from this text, "You will be driving down one of those roads, in 130 degrees Fahrenheit, and you will see two Somali women walking their camels across the scorching-hot desert. They will stop to milk their camels and drink a bit of warm camel milk, but you know they are dying of thirst."

Now, it is natural for humans anywhere to be amazed at how other humans live on this planet. If I was to tell fellow Somalis and/or Africans about extreme cold weather conditions in Canada, they too could be amazed and question the physical characteristics of people who live under these conditions. But, in reality, Mr. Swan is using extreme weather conditions to differentiate Somalis from Canadians, and begins to construct what Hall (1981) would refer to as mapping his worldview in relation to what he sees as a primitive, nomadic, inferior culture so he can continue articulating colonial discourse to re-colonize Somalis in this new land. Much like Margaret Laurence (1988) does in *The Prophet's Camel Bell* that was being reprinted in Canada when Somalis started coming to Toronto.

Mr. Swan continues with his imperial assault, stating that "the Somali physical environment creates the Somali national culture, which is marked by a strong sense of independence...as well as an obsession with family and clan [life]". Mr. Swan is quoted here talking about clan life, with a limited understanding of it, and yet he states that it is great for nomads. However, he gives a very simplistic reason to advance his colonial agenda: "if you have to follow the rain and walk 100 miles from your home, at least if you find someone of your clan, you have a place to pitch your tent for the night."

In a later section of the article, Mr. Swan continues fragmenting the Somali identity by dismissing the importance of clan life when he begins talking about how some Somalis can name their paternal ancestors "some 150 years ago". Thus, the rich ancestral history that all Somalis embody stands out, despite the fact that Mr. Swan is trying to negate and severely undermine clan life. This is very much like Mr. Brown in Achebe's novel when he negates kinship by turning Christian family members against non-Christians by telling them to forget their ancestral ways of life, and to forget clan life (Achebe, 1996). Now, in all fairness, Mr. Swan could be well read in his own family's history, but I doubt that he can speak of his ancestors going back 150 years ago, because, if he could, he would not be amazed that ordinary Somalis can do so. Mr. Swan ends his attack on Somali clan values by placing clan life and tribalism at the heart of the Somali civil conflict, saying: "Now [tribalism is] used to define who you are the enemy of rather than who you belong to." Mr. Swan speaks thus to oversimplify the conflict in Somalia as being a conflict rooted in tribalism. Ngugi Wa Thiong'o (1985), in Decolonizing the Mind: The Politics of Language in African Literature, explains that all conflicts are misrepresented as being simple conflicts between Tribe A versus Tribe B, without looking at colonially imposed factors of wars by the West.

Mr. Swan turns on the community and finally shows his true intentions when he too dismisses Mrs. Anab Osman's refugee claim. As such, Mr. Swan goes on to say, "Nobody would be sent to a foreign embassy that was not highly placed within the Somali ruling class," thus affirming the author's perception that Mrs. Anab Osman's refugee claim is fraudulent. By doing so, Mr. Swan, a Baptist Minister standing in for Christian humanitarianism, pulls that rug from under Somali refugees and dismisses their claim for compassion/ humanitarian assistance. Sadly enough, he does not stop there, even though his allegations are baseless. In fact, he goes on to say that "it is fair to say that refugees who come here are the ones with money and that, in the last 2 years, the Canadian government has worked out a system to allow the nomadic people to come". With such comments, Mr. Swan essentially creates an opportunity for the author to shift the discussion from subhuman nomads who are naturally problematic, to fraudulent refugee claimants who pose an imminent threat to Canadian people and their way of life.

Somalis and the Discourse of Integration

I would like now to utilise Peter Li's (2003) work, *Deconstructing Canada's Discourse of Immigration integration*. Li examines mainstream Canadian immigration debates and discourses. He suggests that the Canadian discourse of integration clearly upholds the normative belief that newcomers should conform to Canadian values, norms and ideals. Moreover, Li points out the contradictions between the discourse of integration and Canada's multicultural immigration policy. Mr. Stoffman's interview with Mr. Nor signifies how the author quotes Mr. Nor articulating the discourse of integration, while presenting him both as an elder and a 'Sheik' in the Somali community.

Mr. Nor is quoted in the beginning of the article saying, "I want Canadian kids to like Somalis because they are gentle and kind... Somalis should dress like Canadians so they can get jobs." This statement shows Mr. Nor articulating integration discourse. Li asserts, "Although the language of integration discourse appears fair to both newcomers and native-born Canadians, it upholds notions of conformity and compliance as a yardstick for evaluating immigrants and expects them to accept prevailing values and beliefs and to acquire living standards and behaviour patterns similar to those of the majority of Canadians" (p. 320). In agreement with Li's (2003) contention, Mr. Nor could innocently have bought into ideals of integration. Yet his statement marginalises Somalis and places a burden on the community to adopt Canadian norms. Additionally, his quote creates a certain image of Mr. Nor as the model Somali newcomer that Somalis need to emulate in order to make it in Canada. The author then goes on to state that Mr. Nor is a Somali elder who wears a *Kofiad*, a Somali cultural hat that men dress in. Drawing on Li's ideas about the discourse of integration, the author's statement signifies that there is room for ethnic diversity with this model. As such, the author's statement portrays an image of a culturally diverse nation for the consumption of the Canadian public, without looking at the wider implications of race and ethnicity in Canadian society.

The author, Mr. Stoffman, goes on to indicate that Mr. Nor was amongst the first arrivals of Somalis in Canada and as a result volunteers at a local Somali community centre that assists new arrivals to make the necessary "transition from Somalis to Canadians." This statement suggests that Mr. Nor has successfully made the transition from Somali to Canadian himself and that he is helping other Somalis make the "transition". The author deliberately makes the above statement to misrepresent the Somali community of Dixon. According to Li (2003):

> It is clear that ethnic enclaves are considered as social features in opposition to "mainstream society" and "broader

community" and therefore at odds with the core values of Canada...At best they are seen as providing a temporary relief to immigrants when they first arrive and as a means of mobilizing resources to overcome barriers...because they encourage "alternative norms, values and behavior. (p. 321)

With this in mind, the author goes on to quote Mr. Nor talking about Somali's organisations using taxpayers' money for their own ends. The author does so to suggest allegations of Canadian taxpayer funding misuse by Somalis.

Moreover, Mr. Nor's comments serve as a double-edged dagger assaulting the Dixon Somali community. On the one hand, Mr. Nor is himself a "member of the [Somali] culture, share[s] sets of concepts, images, ideas which enable him to think and feel about the world, and thus to interpret the world, in roughly similar ways [through]...'cultural codes'" (Hall, 1997. p. 4). Thus, he understands how Somalis operate and can speak about how Somalis function. On the other hand, he is an integrated Westernized Somali who understands how the Canadian system works and therefore can critique the Somali community from a Canadian perspective.

To further misrepresent the Somali community, the author quotes Mr. Nor saying that he is "seeing the kind of cronyism and incompetence on the part of Canadian officials that he thought he had left behind when he fled the war-torn Somalia...I don't understand whether we are in Somalia or in Canada." By placing this quotation that was uttered by a Somali the author is trying to allege that cronyism and incompetence is an inherent characteristic of the nomadic/backward Somalis and has no place in the White Canadian nation space. The above statement makes the explicit allegation that Somalis have "irreconcilable values" that threaten Canada's cohesion by undermining the values of democracy and freedom... [These] cultural differences are seen as essential and unbridgeable and as eventually leading to a clash with the basic values of civil society" (Li, 2003, p.322). Moreover, it affirms pathology of the Somali people and nation, that both are in shambles.

Asserting Whiteness to Mask Racism

I will now turn my attention to Stuart Hall's (1981) work, *The Whites of their Eyes* to analyse how the author of the *Toronto Life* article articulates anti-immigrant and anti-Black discourse. I will first focus on Hall's (1981) critical analysis of the media. Stuart Hall not only deconstructs media programming in the UK through a historical, anti-colonial lens, but also analyses modern-day race conflicts through the same lens. In addition, I feel that it is appropriate to draw on Stuart Hall's work at this point, because Stuart Hall (1981), with his article, was trying to respond to racist colonial ideology that is prevalent in British media.

After the author of the *Toronto Life* article dehumanizes Somalis through the three conversations that I have analysed, he takes a position of journalistic authority and begins articulating anti-immigrant/ anti-Black discourse from a racist "common sense" perspective (Hall, 1981, p. 14). The journalist fuels racial tensions in the Dixon community as a problem of "there are too many Blacks over here" (Hall, 1981, p.19). He does so by referring to the "problem" in the Dixon community as being a "problem of overcrowding". The author also manages to reflect on a conversation that he had with a non-Somali Dixon resident, named Rosette Kertesz, who had met with Sergio Marchesi, Immigration Minister at the time, to do something about this problem, and was asked by the Minister whether she was having problems with Somalis "because they're Black". In the author's attempts to put his own spin on the "Somali problem," he goes as far as suggesting that Somalis have tuberculosis and are infesting the Dixon community with the disease by drawing a health official's concerns into his article. Essentially, by collecting racially loaded narratives, the writer is trying to legitimise his racism.

The author then goes on to restage the stand-off between racist White tenants of Dixon and Somalis in the documentary film "**A Place Called Dixon**," with Mr. Stoffman, as a White journalist, representing the establishment. However, unlike in the documentary film, the author of the *Toronto Life* article declares that the issues in Dixon are not White versus Black. His statement reinforces the dominance of Whiteness in this encounter, and it creates a socially constructed power relationship that is based on imperial domination by Whites of non-White bodies (Hall, 1981).

The author then goes on to draw on the philosophies of Samuel Phillips Huntington (1993) and his arguments on the clash of civilizations, to carry on the author's colonial conquest and to reinforce his imperialist views. Now the introduction of a clash of civilizations gives the author more manoeuvring power in which he, a White man, can set up psychological battle for the readers and then lead the expedition as a colonizer to tilt the scales in favour of his views. He does so by precisely dismissing racial tensions in the community as a "two-way street" by indicating that "Dixon management has had to clean up anti-White graffiti from the swimming pool and parking lots on several occasions."

Now, by writing about these alleged incidents the author, as a "reporter" is using his credentials and social status to interpret the incidents from a White viewpoint to implicate his subjects, in agreement with Hall's (1981) idea of imperial discourse. How else could he come to the conclusion that Somalis are responsible for anti-White graffiti? I mean, there are other non-White residents in the community. He does not give readers any indication as to when the graffiti had to be cleaned up (before or after the Somalis moved into Dixon), assuming any vandalism actually took place. But, again, the author is using his position to implicate Somalis before his readers, and isn't too concerned with uncovering the truth.

To give his allegations of Somali racism some weight, the author draws on the narratives of a Somali woman in a book called *Aman: the Story of a Somali Girl*, written by Virginia Lee Barnes and Janice Boddy (1994). First, he calls it a very "fascinating book," then he goes on to state that "Whites are considered dirty in Somalia because they aren't circumcised and they don't wash after using the toilet". Yet what is ironic about it is the fact that he is equating circumcision in his article with cleanliness, and he is not taking it up to "save Somali women" discourse from circumcision, like traditional Western media when it comes to this issue. What this shows is that the author is drawing on a complex colonial ideology that is based on a social relation that transforms discourse and creates a subject that is at the author's disposal for his colonial history (Hall, 1981). Now it is interesting that the author does not have to be consistent in his re-articulation of colonial discourse to marginalise his subject.

In the same section of the article, the author also uses quotes from *Aman: the Story of a Somali Girl* to paint Somalis as being prejudice towards other Blacks. He does so by stating that "the word *'adone'*, meaning slave in Somali, is often used to describe other Africans with darker skin or coarser hair." To give this claim more legitimacy, he says, "The word was routinely applied in Mogadishu to Sir Victor Gbeho, the Ghanaian who was the United Nations special representative there until the UN pulled out last March." In essence, the author is using what Hall (1981) calls the "grammar of race," in which the discursive and power coordination is historically constructed through imagery, stereotypes, and racial characteristics. Because the author is occupying the position of colonial master in the article, he has the power to juxtapose two African peoples' narratives against one another so that he can essentially make his arguments. I say this because I am not so sure whether Sir Gbeho, a fellow African, would have agreed to have his name used in this article. Nevertheless, the fact that his name is in the article and his physical features are used to paint a negative picture of Somalis, allows the reader to draw very negative conclusions about communities' prejudices.

The final section of this article that I am going to examine, is subtitled Welfare. The author essentially uses this section to end his article with classical colonial confrontation in which "the natives always move as anonymous mass-in tribes or hordes. And against them is always a counterpoised White figure, alone 'out there' confronting his Destiny or shouldering his Burden in the 'heart of darkness', displaying coolness under fire and an unshakeable authority" (Hall, 1981, p.16). The author does this by first introducing Lyn McLeod, the Ontario Liberal Leader of the time, who accused Somalis of committing welfare fraud, and called Somalis, in a legislative section, "Desert Gypsies". In this case, Lyn McLeod signifies the White authority figure that is taking on the Somalis as they invade the "White Canadian nation space" as Hall (1981) would argue. After the author brings in this politician to the article, he begins referring to some outrageous figures that incriminate Somalis of perpetrating welfare fraud. The author does not end it there. In fact, he quotes another unidentified "government expert," who wishes to remain anonymous in his article, saying "Somali welfare abuse in Ontario amounts to one million dollars a month," and the author precisely does so to make Lyn McLeod's allegation stick. In essence, these accusations create a violent struggle in which the invading Somalis need to be confronted, in concert with Hall's (1981) ideas of the media's imaginative colonial encounters.

Secondly, the author reintroduces Mr. Nor, the controversial Somali figure, who misrepresented Somalis earlier on in this article to stand in for the Somali invaders once gain in agreement with what Hall's (1997) ideas of representation. In a very ironic twist, the author refers to a moment where Mr. Nor essentially pulls out his wallet to show the author his Canadian citizen card. The author then tells Mr. Nor: "Don't let anybody treat you like a second-class citizen" and Mr. Nor responds by saying "that is right". At that moment, Mr. Nor turns from "being a native with a primitive nobility and simple dignity [to] a savage... and restless native that is threatening to over-run the [Country]." (Hall, 1981, p 15). This conversation is used by the author to construct a stand-off between the Canadian White nation state and the "nomadic Somalis" that are invading it by using Mr. Nor to represent Somalis. In addition, this conversation speaks to the urgency to get the "Somali problem" out of Canada, a problem that was echoed by every White body in this article. The deliberate misrepresentation of the Somali voice in this article also denies Somalis the ability to put up any resistance to colonization.

Fallen Stars

I have vivid memories of the Somali community's sentiment when this article was published. My family owned and operated one of a handful of Somali restaurants in Toronto located at the corner of Runnymede and St. Clair streets called Dallo Restaurant. It was at work that I found out about this article and essentially obtained a copy. Our family restaurant was located in the heart of Toronto's Somali business district and there were a few local shops, restaurants, and Somali cafes in the vicinity. Everyone in the community was up in arms over this article, and especially disturbed by Mr. Nor's comments. Therefore, I had decided to attain a copy to read this article. SO I asked a regular patron of our restaurant, named Hassan, for his copy. At first I was in a state of panic as Hassan handed me the magazine and I was so sure that I wanted to read it. But then I thought to myself how I can ever tell the story of being Somali in the Canadian landscape when the day comes if I don't confront injustice by reading this article. I was also overcome with an overwhelming sense of responsibility, as powerless as I was at the time, to witness the injustice that was being done to my community. As a Somali, I was brought up to believe in the power of standing witness before an injustice and to physically, emotionally, and psychologically confront it; moreover, to wait for the day when telling the story of the injustices that took place. As a matter fact, I am having an "Ah ha" moment, a moment of clarity, not only because I indeed survived the article, but because this work, I now have a chance to critically interrogate this article and tell the story of my community.

After I received the magazine, I situated myself in a quiet corner where I could see everyone in the restaurant because deep down in me, I knew that racism was merciless and therefore I had no desire to feel alone with this article. In addition, just a few days prior to the publication of this article, a CTV media crew was at the Somali café that is two doors away from our restaurant to interview Somalis about the conduct of the Canadian soldiers in Somalia[3]. I was utterly disturbed by how race was dismissed as a motivating factor of the crimes that were committed by the Canadian Airborne Regiment against unsuspecting Somalis.

As I began reading the article, I took notice of Mr. Nor's picture in the article and I was shocked to find out that he was the man the community had said ran his mouth afoul. As my innocent eyes meet his quotes, I began to feel the pain of his words and then I recalled seeing Mr. Nor wearing full Somali regalia two nights prior to reading this article. I did not know what to make of his statements. I had known this individual because he frequented our restaurant. But his words were far from being Somali, and based on my experience, no elder and/or Sheik would have ever said those words. As I read on, the sense of betrayal and humiliation were unbearable.

Although as a youth I couldn't fully comprehend the colonial/anti-immigration agenda behind the article, my embodied knowledge as a Somali made me realise that this article was the colonizer's interpretation of the Somali peoples. I was able to quickly distance myself from the author's attack because of his careless introduction, "Somalia is a tropical land of camel herders". My embodied knowledge created a resilient moment of defiance in the face of colonial aggression and it allowed me to conceptualise the article for what it was. As such, Mr. Swan's, voice was typical of the missionaries, that the Elders in the community often spoke about, who would not be satisfied until every Somali was subject of Her Majesty the Queen of England. I was more disgusted than surprised with the author's views. However, I was debilitated and hurt by Mr. Nor's words - a man whom I saw wearing full regalia just days before. I could not reconcile these two opposing pictures: on one hand, in my youthful

---

3   The Somalia Affair was a <u>Canadian</u> military scandal in the mid-1990s. It began with the brutal 1993 beating death of a Somali teenager, <u>Shidane Arone</u>, at the hands of two Canadian soldiers participating in the <u>United Nations</u> humanitarian efforts in <u>Somalia</u>. The crime, documented by grizzly photos, shocked the Canadian public and brought to light internal problems in the Canadian Airborne Regiment that went beyond the two soldiers directly involved.

understanding, he embodied the institution of *Odaynemuo* [Somali Eldership], but now, on the other hand, he was marginalising the community and not speaking like an Elder. Consequently, I decided to go to Dixon to hear the Somali communal voice and to *wardoon* [find the full story] of the community. Slowly my anger, frustration, and fragmentation turned to a desire to be healed and rescued from drowning in colonial discourse and the only place in which I could go and get healing was at Dixon itself.

When I got to Dixon, what I saw there transformed my soul forever. As I entered the space between the 230 and the 340 buildings, I saw large gatherings of Somalis, mainly adults and Elders. My spirit was immediately uplifted when I saw the scene. I felt a calling to be part of that collective, and I was amazed to see the gathering, because I had not seen such a sight ever since I left Somalia a few years earlier. Everybody was gathered in circles; some people were standing, others were sitting down. As I walked closer towards the crowds, I noticed that there was a big circle in which everyone was sitting and there was a middle aged man standing in the middle of it, addressing the crowd. So I joined that circle and as I listened in, I heard him say *"Haybad waxaanu kulaneyn dulkeeunii Hooyo"* [We have pride in the land of our mother]. When I heard those words, I lost myself in my emotions and all of a sudden did not feel out of place. Those words were paraphrased from Abdi Bahire (1977) song *Dalkaaga Hooyo*. As a child I used to hear this nationalist song all over Somali radio, and I was mesmerized when I was reminded of it again. *Dolqaga Hyoo* is a song that talks about the importance of nationhood and pride in being Somali. This simple phrase, *"Haybad waxhn qulanahy dolqana hoyoo,"* encapsulates the story of my exile. For me, an individual nobody is anything outside his homeland. More importantly, it connected me with my *dhaqan* [culture], history, and Somaliness. It reminded me of how things were back home. Therefore, I became, in that congregation, part of a collective voice that was resisting colonization.

I remember walking away from that circle full of hope and life and I joined a small group of men and women standing together. I stood next to them as one of the men said, *"Xalimooy Gabadhaa yare e aan gacanta kuhayo ayaa ummadda isu keeni doonta. Nur waa ragii gumeysiga la shaueyn jray"* [Halimo, do you see my little daughter, her generation will bring the nation together. Nor is just like those old men who worked for colonists.] This statement connected me with my embodied history as a colonized person colonial past were the colonizers often used some native to work against their own communities. Hawa Jibril (2008), the legendary Somali oral traditionalist in her 1962 *burambur* [composed orality] called *Odeyaash Ina Akhiray* [The Old Men Who Hold Us Back] offers an explanation of the actions of Mr. Nor as being the actions of the old men who collaborated with colonialists when she wrote:

Urur ma yesshan oo, arrin meelna kuma furan
Eheladoodana ajnabigay, Ka jecel yihiin
Miyaan la arkaynin, odayaasha ina akhiray
Asaaggen innaga reebe, ee ha larga ilboxo (p. 150)

English translation:

United they are not, nor have they a common purpose
To their fellow brothers, they prefer the foreigners.
Don't you see these old men?
Who hold us back?
Let them not prevail over us.

Additionally, this statement sets a new course for me as a Somali youth to be part of a new generation of Somalis who will change the face of the Somali nation. I never felt so resilient in my whole life. Reading the article was painful but yet hearing the Somali narrative constructed in the place called Dixon not only began the process of healing for me. In addition, it also awakened a consciousness in me to take part in the struggle of my people against colonial aggression.

Conclusion

Having an opportunity to respond to this article from a Somali perspective has been something that I have wanted to do for a long time. Looking back on **"Dispatch from Dixon,"** thirteen years after this article was first published; it has been a journey for me, at times painful, at times humiliating, and at times disempowering. Yet have waited a long time for the opportunity to critically respond to this article. When I first started writing this chapter, I was hesitant and even felt incapable of explicating this interrogating. I often found myself fragmented and drowning in my desire to break free from the colonial/racializing discourses that are dominant in this article. I came face-to-face with some of the most degrading literature ever written about

Somalis in Canada. In addition, it brought back some memories that I'd rather forget. Nevertheless, it was a necessary journey. I had to revisit the past that I embodied as a Somali in the Canadian landscape in order to tell my story of being branded an uncivilized, undeserving Somali refugee. This journey has brought me closer to a place where I can begin to bring some closure to a painful chapter in my life and to begin a healing process. Now that I have had the time to reflect on the community's journey, I will now narrate some of my schooling experiences in the following chapter to bring another painful chapter of my life to closure.

Chapter 4
Colonial Education and the Self

Background

In this chapter, I narrate some of my stories to theorise some of my lived experiences with colonial education in the Canadian landscape. I have purposely chosen this particular form of expression to describe the realities and experiences of Somali-Canadian youth, as I speak about my own story of survival as a Somali male at the margins of the larger Canadian society. This chapter speaks of my journey in the education system. As a 'budding' scholar in one of the world's leading academic institutions, this narrative is at once a burden and a responsibility that requires courage and resourcefulness to contest Eurocentric privileging and rigid academic structures.

In this chapter I will narrate some of my own schooling experiences for they speak to the deep psychological and spiritual scars that I embody as a racialized Somali. I will critically examine these topics with the aim of theorising my "lived experiences," as Dei (2008) would say. I will then engage in self-reflection to show how I utilised elements of my Somali *dhaqan* to escape the constant colonial gaze. I will conclude by arguing that establishing African-centric schools is essential to the holistic development and sustainability of the '*Say-Walahi*' generation of youth in particular and the Somali community in general.

I attended Silverthorne Collegiate Institute, a predominantly White high school in a rich upper middle class neighbourhood. Every morning as I entered my high school, I was confined to an identity that was inescapable. Through no fault of my own, I was marked as an unwanted Somali refugee who was invading White Canadian space. While some saw my Somali-ness through media-formed visions of famine, others viewed me as an undeserving "Third-World" subject, infesting Canadian society. I am overcome with anxiety, sadness, and frustration as I begin writing about the education system that deformed my identity and devalued my ancestral ways of knowing. By revisiting issues that I had laid to rest in the depth of my psyche, some which still linger in the shadows of my character, I hope that the examination of my colonial education will bring me to a place of resolution. My aim is to enter into a place of healing from which I can create visions of a brighter future for the '*Say-Walahi*' generation.

As a Somali-Canadian teenager, the mid- to late 1990s were especially difficult. This period coincided with the high point of the Somali civil war. The growing anti-Somali sentiment in the GTA made life as a racialized person even more unbearable. The greatest injustice that was ever inflicted upon me was being constantly reminded of "Canada's peacekeeping" machine in my classrooms. As a Black youth, I was also automatically labelled as dysfunctional learner who was incapable of succeeding academically, due to "cultural deficiencies" that I was often told that I had. As a displaced African, I occupy a peculiar space: I seek to move beyond an academic exercise to ultimately re-imagine schooling from an African-centric perspective, with a holistic approach to learning and knowing. My lived experience has ignited the desire to take a critical look at the education system.

Colonial Education and the Self

In my first year of high school, at Silverthorne C.I., was one of only three Somali students who had attended the school. It was a very tense time in my school life. The "Canadian peacekeeping machine" scandal was all over the news, reports of Somalis' being welfare scammers were frequently headlined, and an intense anti-immigration debate was going on as Canada's population of racialized minorities grew rapidly. Going through high school in such a political climate was a very difficult one. However, I was somewhat invisible as a Somali in my first year of high school. I had no recognizable accent, and most of the White people in my school had never met a Somali. Therefore, I was able to escape the colonial gaze. Every so often, I would hear someone make dehumanizing comments about Somalis, and my stomach would churn. Amongst so many White bodies, I often felt very isolated. Subsequently I retreated to having conversations with myself in my *afkeyga hooyo* [mother language].

During my second year in high school, as many as seventy Somali students enrolled. In addition, **"Dispatch from Dixon,"** was also published, and anti-Somali sentiment was at an all-time high. Everything was rapidly changing for the worse: Somali-ness, in my school, was construed as being synonymous with violence and criminality. Dei *et al* (1997), in his ethnographic study of Black youth, captured this reality by stating that "[Black] students... complained about the social stereotyping of Black males as 'violent,' as 'troublemakers' and even as 'criminals'" (p. 116). I remember during the second week of school overhearing the principal, Mrs.

Wright, telling a group of Somali male students during lunchtime to "stay out of trouble...this is a country of peace." I recall going over to these students as the principal walked away and, because I knew that they did not speak English, asking them, "*Maxay idinku tiri diritooradu?*" [What did the principal want from you?], to which one of them replied, "*Wayiska hadlaysay*" [She was just talking to us]. I had never seen Mrs. Wright in such a mood. But it seems that she was responding to an imaginary racial crisis, which Hall (1981) refers to as "the immigration problem [being] the number of Blacks is too high" (p. 20). It is with this attitude that the principal and school administration kept policing the hallways.

After that incident, I became more vigilant and kept a watchful eye. Tensions in the school kept mounting between the White students, teachers, administrators, and the Somali student body. We began to feel like we were constantly under surveillance and that almost every White person would talk down to us. I especially noticed how the teachers' attitudes towards me had changed from my first year to my second year. Although I was well aware of how the Somali identity was being taken up in Canadian society, I was quite surprised by how teachers in my classes began ignoring me and singling me out as a troublesome, underachiever. Dei *et al* (1997) offers an explanation:

> [There is an] unwritten code that might be understood as part of the 'hidden curriculum' of schooling through which attitudes and behaviours of teachers and other school agents convey specific messages to students...many Black students feel that these messages are often conveyed through a climate of preconceptions which are fuelled by racial stereotypes. (p. 72)

This mind-set caused my homeroom teacher, Mr. Young, to suggest that I make an appointment to see the school guidance counsellor. According to Mr. Young, "I was not myself lately, and I needed to seek some counselling." So I decided to take his advice, and I set an appointment to see the guidance counsellor the next day. As soon as I walked into the office of Mr. Brown, the guidance counsellor, I noticed him looking me up and down with a look of utter disgust. I remember thinking, "This is a strange welcome!" Mr. Brown told me to have a seat, so I did. Then he began a humiliating interrogation process by asking me very personal questions: When did I come to Canada? How old was I when I left my homeland [Somalia]? Are all my family members in Canada? Are my parents together? What is my immigration status? He even went so far as to ask whether my immunization was up to date and whether I had an OHIP card. Yet this man had all my public school records in a file on his desk. I remember shrinking in my seat and thinking to myself *Warya kan Kugusoo Kalihyey Saka?* [What made you come to this so early in the morning?].

Dei and Asgharadeh (2001) describe the interrogation process that I was subjected to as the "'shark phenomenon' which is a practice that see[s] subjects merely as 'objects and subjects'...This practice is seeking only to (re)produce colonial relations and power relations" (p. 70). As Mr. Brown's dehumanizing interrogation was drawing to an end, he had the audacity to ask me if I had any questions for him. At that moment, I remember courageously collecting myself and resiliently rupturing the racializing/colonizing efforts of this man by asking him, "Are you a medical doctor, an immigration officer, or a school counsellor?" because I felt so violated. In reaction to my question, he proceeded to tell me, "I'm only here to help you. Some of the Somali students are having problems at school." After I heard him say that, I remember thinking *"Kalye Anegae ea waale"* [Come, drive me crazy]. I decided not to prolong the discussion any further and kept quiet. With my silence, I was resisting "cultural hegemony of [White] society, which maintains legitimacy by reproducing a silent discourse, based on the negative construction of Otherness" (Dei et al., 1997, p. 231).

Soon enough, my school began feeling like a psychological prison in which the Somali student body was being constantly subjugated. During the first semester of my Grade 10 year, it felt like none of the White people wanted us at their school. No matter what we did, we could not escape feeling unwanted and unworthy. Some of us were pressured into taking meaningless cultural-sensitivity classes, and Somali students were being constantly disciplined for "breaking the rules." All the White authority figures were using language that defined Somali students as violent and constantly told us, "This is Canada. Now you can't be violent." The process of simultaneous hypervisibility (Dei, 2008) of Somali bodies was inescapable: A process that encoded us as criminal and deviant, while also negating our histories and experiences.

Moreover, the White students began harassing Somali students regularly, and we were being called "f***ing Somalis" on a daily basis. So fights between Somali and White students became a norm in the school. Somali students made countless complaints about being treated unfairly and being picked on by White students, who often addressed them with racial slurs. But the White school staff and administration never took our complaints seriously at all. The fighting escalated. When there was a major fight between a few Somalis and a few Whites, the whole school administration went into an uproar and the Somali students were blamed for all the fighting.

To our astonishment, the Somali students who were involved in the fighting got longer suspensions than their White opponents. All Somali students in the school received a letter to take home, about the school's policy on violence and it was our "violent culture" that was blamed for all the fighting. As such, the school's White authority figures claimed that the school was "peaceful until Somalis came to the school". Soon enough "f***ing Somalis" turned into "you f***ing Somalis go back home." To add insult to injury, one day all the Somali students were summoned to the school auditorium and asked to sit in one section of it. As we were assembling in the auditorium, the school principal, one of the vice-principals, and a police officer were observing us. They were whispering back and forth to one another, and there was a cameraman videotaping us as well. I remember feeling the intensity of emotion in the room and being overwhelmed with anger and frustration. The power relations in that auditorium were crystal clear. We were the racialized Somali student body, and they were the White authority figures. I did not know how to understand what was happening, because I had never been confronted by White supremacy in my school like this before, and I did not know what to make of it. Hall (1997) would argue that my inability to process the situation was as a result of unfamiliarity with "[a] system and conventions of representation, the code of their [White] language and culture, which equip them with cultural know-how, enabling them to function [in a society]" (p. 22).

The principal, Mrs. Wright then started speaking. The first words that came out of her mouth were, "I'm sure many of you have heard me say this before." As soon as she said that, I knew that she was going to reinforce the dominance of White culture on us. She went on, "This is Canada. You should not be violent and behave like you don't have any rules." At that moment I remember detaching myself from being captive in the auditorium and daydreaming about escaping racial injustice. The humiliating interrogation lasted for 45 minutes, but seemed like it went on for eternity. Little did I know,

I was learning about the "power of Whiteness... to be 'safe' it was important to recognise the power of Whiteness...to fear it, and to avoid encountering it" (hooks, 1997, p. 175). This was a valuable lesson that would, indeed, serve me well in a White school and that still governs my every action as I navigate the academy as a graduate student. Now that I reflect back on that encounter, I begin to grasp the profound impact it had on me. I am besieged by the realisation that, less than a handful of the Somali males who were present in that meeting actually graduated from high school. Dei *et al* (1997), in reconstructing the drop-out phenomenon, would argue that the Somali students were pushed out. I even remember having to transfer schools to get my high school diploma during my final year.

Cultural Resiliency and a Fragmented Existence

From that day in which the Somali students were summoned to the auditorium, I decided never to be cornered by Whiteness again and to actively resist all White authority figures. I had seen what multiculturalism and tolerance looked like in my high school. I was convinced that in order to get through high school, I had to use my ancestral *dhaqan,* because not graduating from high school was just not an option for me. As such, my parents would have never allowed me to not complete high school. The thought of being constantly exposed to a discourse that associated my culture and identity "with low status, humiliation, corporal punishment, slow-foot intelligence and ability or downright stupidity, non-intelligence and barbarism" (Wa Thiong'o, 1985, p.18), was illogical. I knew that all those stereotypes did not accurately represent my identity. I also knew that I was facing racism and that, if I did not defy it, it would socially deform me, and then ultimately break me. This was a profound realisation, and it allowed me to understand the negative power of racism. As the Somali proverb goes, "*Biyoo kaabadan iyo dad kaabadanba wey kuhafiyaan* [a large body of water, as well as a people of majority, will drown you]". Therefore, I decided to isolate myself from everything non-Somali and non-African in the school and to create a space in which my Somali culture was at the centre of my existence rather than on the periphery.

It seemed like there was an unwritten code of resistance that Somali students, especially the males, abided by after our experience in the auditorium. We collectively decided to become one Somali student body and we took up Somali culture to survive in the school. This new mode of resistance made school a little more tolerable.

It also made it easier to dismiss the White authority figures and strategically escape their detection. Again Dei *et al* (1997) in their ethnographic study offer an explanation:

> Students gave the impression that [there is a] sense of validation which is derived from having Black students ... Black friends made school a more tolerable experience and, literally, helped them get through the day. This aspect of 'surviving the system' pervades their school experiences. Indeed, Black students share strategies of coping with each other which can be instrumental to their school success. (p. 155)

We, as young Black men, knew that we were against a system that was designed solely to deprive us from achieving any meaningful endeavour in our lives. Somali culture made it easier for me to function in school with a complete self. It enabled me to be part of a collective identity that was wholesome and complete. This sense of self created interconnectedness amongst the Somali students, and it provided me with a cultural safety net. Through this support system, I was able to go to school and hold my head up high and to the best of my ability completely separate myself from White supremacy. I observed complete silence when I was not amongst Somalis and kept my contact with Whites to a minimum, because I was aware of the power of Whiteness and confronting Whiteness was something that I could not do.

Soon enough, I recognised the power of expressing my Somali *dhaqan* knowledges in my internal conversations with the self at school, to oppose the colonization/racialization. These conversations took place in my *Afkeyga Hooyo* [mother tongue] and were a deliberate act of agency and resistance. I always thought in my *Afkeyga Hoyo* prior to the auditorium experiences, but ever since the Dixon communal experience that I highlighted in chapter three, my Somali consciousness had developed in strength and character, thus allowing me to carry myself in the face of Whiteness. This internal consciousness had a voice that was vibrant in me and it allowed me to converse with myself. It is through this voice that I was not only able to hear myself, but also able to unlock the Somali-ness that was in my soul. Indeed these internal conversations were different from any of my previous ones because they allowed me to fully embody my culture. What was most profound for me as a young Somali was the fact that my own conversations connected me with other Somali voices in my life. For instance, I would often hear the voices of my parents, Elders, and the community within my conversations. Wa Thiong'o (1985) describes language "as not a mere string of words. It ha[s] power well beyond the immediate and lexical meaning...languages, through images and symbols, give us a view of the world" (p. 11). My thoughts created a cultural utopia that allowed me to escape cultural domination, colonizing knowledges, and White authority. These conversations in my *Afkeyga Hooyo* allowed me to regain my full humanity from colonial ideology and racialization. Furthermore, they heightened both my awareness of and attachment to my ancestral community and homeland. These thoughts encompassed Somali cultural know-how, histories, landscape, proverbs, poems, spirituality, and acts of imaginary escape. Most importantly, I was the only one aware of my resistance, because it took place in my cultural psyche.

Somali *dhaqan* came in handy, especially in my high school classes, where I was often the only racialized body. Whenever a racist comment was made in class and/or my culture was put down, I would dismiss these slurs with an internal conversation comprising a Somali proverb, oralilty, and/or song. These acts were so powerful for me, especially when it came to history seen through the dominant lens, because these acts provided me with images, perspectives, and connected me to ancestral homeland. What was even more profound about my internal conversations is that they gave me an avenue for separating myself from the immediate colonial environment and imagining community life before the colonial encounter.

I would be in a classroom in Toronto and find myself in *Nugaal* or *Howed*, my ancestral homeland, standing in front of *Ceelka Awaoayashy* [waterwheel of the forefathers]. Or walking through the streets of *Xamar* [Mogadishu], as I remembered it and not as it was being misrepresented by mainstream media. At times though, I would be so overpowered by colonial knowledge and find myself suffering from what hook (1997) refers to as "White fatigue," particularly when it came to discussions of how the "Canadian peacekeeping" machine was often taken up in my classes. At those times, I would often walk out of class to catch my breath and to take a moment to reflect on what I had just experienced. If I was lucky, I would run into a fellow Somali and could begin a conversation with him/her. Other times, I would be beleaguered by fragmentation and find myself in the *Geedka Hoostiisa* [beneath the Acacia tree] somewhere in Somalia, pondering social, political, and cultural questions. *Geedka Hoostiisa* is an institutional pillar of the Somali culture representing the collective psyche of the community. It embodies tradition, spirituality, and an intergenerational connectedness; it is a place where all community ceremonies take place, community issues are addressed, and conflicts are resolved. This concept is essentially in the style of town hall, signifying a communal, social and political way of life. It is also space where community members can collectively unlock the knowledges, histories, and legacies that they embody. I asked myself, "How did we get to this point? What happened? And why?" I would try to reconstruct the identity of the Somali people – my people before colonialism, civil war, famine, and displacement. *Geedka Hoostiisa* essentially represents a forum for discussion in the style of a town hall which is, it is communal, social and political. It is also a space where community members can collectively unlock their knowledges, histories, and legacies that they embody.

To truly counter the social formative processes that have racialized me, it became crucial to embrace my culture and cultivate it in my life. According to Hall (1990), we need to think of cultural identity as something that is never complete and always in process within us. My process of cultural reproduction allows me to exist in Canada as an Indigenous African traveller, who is on a journey to find belonging and is constantly resisting loss of identity. Although my cultural reclamation process was triggered by my encounter with colonization, it has nevertheless fuelled my desire for complete decolonization as an adult.

Cultural identity comes from one's particular geographic location, and it also comes with a history that is constantly changing (Hall, 1990). It was this constant change that allowed me to reassemble my cultural identity while living in Canada most of my life. I did so by collecting Somali regalia and wearing it on appropriate occasions. Most Somalis I came across did not know that I grew up in the GTA. Therefore, they did not know my history and could not question the authenticity of my Somali-ness. Moreover, most Somalis saw me as a newcomer who was more authentic than other members of the Somali diaspora. To my parents and close family members, however, I was just being weird, and they could not understand why I was so eager to dress in traditional Somali regalia, even though I was a teenager whenever I got a chance. To me, I was experiencing my culture through the clothing I wore. These experiences allowed me to construct my own world as I wanted it to be. I was able to pick out various aspects of my North Somali culture, romanticize them, and freeze that experience in a cultural utopia to which no one else had access (Hall, 1990). This creativity allowed me to conceptualise Somalia as a wonderful place that I could rediscover time and again by travelling as a nomad, to connect to my roots as I imagined them. This is a process that Hall (1990) calls "imaginary reunification" (p. 224). It is a process that members of African diasporas, dispersed across the globe through slavery and colonialism, use to resist fragmentation and displacement. For me, the process of imaginary reunification created a sense of belonging. It empowered me to construct a decolonized selfhood rooted in a culture, homeland, and communal existence free from domination, subjugation and dehumanization.

African-centred Schooling and Hope

As a displaced African who has spent most of his life in exile, I conceptualise African-centred school as a place of belonging, but more importantly as a place for renewal and re-birth for the youth who have been colonized, racialized, and 'Otherized'. As a student that has gone through a colonial/racializing education system, I have longed for an education system that "plac[es] African ideals at the centre of any analysis that involves African culture and behaviour" (Asante, 1998, p.8). Thoughts of African-centred schooling take me back to a time when I was relatively free, when I belonged to a community and was part of a collective psyche. When I think of African-centred schools, I think of the *Dugsi* educational system, where Somali children learn the Holy Quran, oral traditions and *dhaqan* in their community. *Dugsi* is a place where children learn about communal life. This system has existed in Somalia for centuries, and it has relatively survived colonialism. Although, it is not institutionalized into the formal education system in Somalia, it continues to be the pillar of our social fabric.

Children go to *Dugsi* when they are about five or six years old, carrying their *loox* [portable wooden writing board]. There is a *Dugsi* in every neighbourhood, so it is accessible to every child and children don't have to walk far. Children are handed over to their *Macalin* [teacher] at that very young age, and brought up to be part of a collective community. In the *Dugsi,* the children are introduced to an " African system of thought...that emphasises that to understand reality is to weave a holistic view of society, that is to accept the need for a harmonious co-existence between nature, culture and society"

(Wane, 2005, p.1). For most children their first day of *Dugsi* is the first day they get exposed to learning outside their home and family. The *Dugsi* has a profound impact on Somali children's social, cultural, and spiritual character and that is why it's not uncommon to hear of a Somali speaking about the *maalintii dugsi la igeeyey* [the day I was taken to *Dugsi*].

The sceptic's question whether the African-centred model of schooling has any relevance to the lives of African-Canadian youth growing up in Canada. My school experiences told in the above narrative is a testament to not only the relevance but also the need of Afro-centred schools. As Asante (1991) asserts, Eurocentric schools dislocate and fragment racialized students, it is crucial to the subsistence of the African-Canadian diaspora to develop African-centric schools that could provide African-Canadian learners with a non-Eurocentric and non-White supremacist school model. It is time to begin imagining a more holistic educational paradigm that accounts for African-Canadian cultures, histories, and we are at a critical juncture wherein the stakes have never been higher and the grips of colonization/racialization have never been more detrimental to our youth. In essence, Asante (1991) would argue, it is time that we give African-Canadian youth a new pair of eyes to see African-centred realities that validate their realities, experiences and sense of being. I concur with Asante's (1998) ideas that we need to think about Africa as a subject location, since Africans have been removed and displaced from Africa through slavery and colonization, it is important for members of the diaspora to think of Africa as a concept of subject location and aspire to an African –centred education from that perspective.

Conclusion

My encounter with colonial education is one that has caused me deep psychological and mental scarring. My schooling experience has been so traumatizing that I have never been able to grasp its impact on my soul. Yet I know that I carried all that pain and suffering within me. I never even had the courage to think about or talk about my story until I was in graduate school at the University of Toronto at Ontario Institute for Studies in Education (OISE). Ironically however, it was at graduate school that I began reflecting on and recollecting all the humiliating moments in my educational life. It was then that I realised that my soul was fragmented and that I needed to speak about my encounter in order to processes the impact of colonial education on me. As such, I now share my story with a vision of hope for a brighter future for the *'Say-Walahi'* generation and future generations of Somali Canadians. It is with this sense of hope that I imagine an African-centred school that situates Somali youth within its education.

Chapter 5

Trauma and Psychological Displacement

In this chapter, I will examine issues of the *'Say-Walahi'* generation's cultural dislocation. My aim is to show the state of identity fragmentation that has resulted from the physical, psychological, and cultural separation of Somali youth from their homeland. As an example, I will analyse a video documentary of the first annual Ohio Youth Summit to discuss this fragmentation and cultural dislocation and to show the extent to which Somali youth have internalised ideologies that dehumanize their Somali identity. Moreover, I will show how processes of internalisation further add injury to their souls. The resultant colonial social construction of the Somali identity has been detrimental to the *'Say-Walahi'* youth as well as to other future generations of Somalis because they have no collective memory of Somalia, Somali *dhaqan*, Somali histories, and Somali society that they can juxtapose to the colonial imagery and discourse. Consequently, they can't see themselves outside the racialized status that has been ascribed to them. What is even more tragic is both international and local discourse of the Somali body is articulated through a Eurocentric hegemonic colonial lens that further dehumanizes the Somali people.

In my analysis I will first conceptualise some of my lived experiences in exile. My aim is not to give the impression that every Somali living in the diaspora has gone through a similar uprooting process and that all Somalis carry narratives of exile, but, rather to utilise my own narrative of dislodgment as I reflect on my own identity struggles as a Somali living in Canada. I will then turn my attention to two presentations made by two Somalis at the summit. I will conclude with a look at the reflections of a Somali youth on the summit and how this youth undergoes an identity transformation while attending the summit.

Images in Exile

I would like to utilise Anthony Shelton's (2000) article, Museum Ethnography: An Imperial Science. In his work Shelton examines the social and cultural processes in which museum objects are used to assign values and meaning to non-European cultures. I have chosen to employ Shelton's (2000) work in order to examine how dehumanizing values were assigned to my Somali identity during the civil war and the resulting famine in the early 1990s. My aim is to contextualise how Western media broadcast images about the events that were unfolding in Somalia and how it felt like my Somali identity was on display as an object of Western interpretation.

"Life is a highway. I wanna ride it all night long," are the words of Canadian rock artist Tom Cochrane from his 1991 single: 'Life is a Highway.' For me this song conjures images of starving Somali children in *Baladwane,* Somalia. Tom Cochrane had made a trip to *Baladwane*, Somalia, along with other celebrities, including former Australian Prime Minister Bob Hawke. Cochrane got a few pictures taken with a severely malnourished Somali child which created an international spectacle to capture images of hunger in the "Dark Continent." This amounts to what is known in the entertainment industry as "media overkill" (Richburg, 1992). Visions of these images are still fresh in my memory. I can see him with his stylish blond hair, blue eyes, holding a starving, bare-chest Somali child. Shelton (2000) would argue that Cochrane took the pictures to show the "exotic object...as a testimonial to the voyages [he has] undertaken and the peculiar culture [that he] encountered" (p.157). He is sitting on the ground covered with desert dust looking at the camera man, posing for the picture. I can feel the anguish and sorrow of nearby Somalis that are settled in a camp nearby where these pictures were being taken. The Somali child in that photo serves as an object...that constitutes, for colonial science and administration, an important index of 'Otherness' (Shelton, 2000, p.158). It is those images that I tried for years to break free from with very little luck. There was a worldwide campaign to capitalise on the "Somali hunger."

Everywhere I turned images of severely malnourished Somalis, especially women and children were on display. I can even remember turning on the television to watch episodes of World Wrestling Federation (WWF) on Saturday mornings only to see wrestlers promoting a 'Headlock on Hunger' campaign raising money for Somalia which contributed to the "empirical functionalism, market[ing] the transition from knowledge seen as a universalising master narrative to its re-articulation as a myriad of discrete constituents of information archive...this reconfiguration of knowledge corresponds to a transition from its symbolic or categorical usage as a means of cultural differentiation to an agent of [subjection]" (Shelton, 2000, p.158). Then there were the video clips of warfare, machine gun fire, and explosions that frequented the evening news. It was relentless and I was utterly disturbed by the violent script that was being ascribed to my homeland and its people. Whenever I was inundated by exposure to these violent images, I often found myself mentally transported back to the gate of my family home in *Xamar [Mugdisho]*, on my last day on Somali soil before my family and I departed to Canada, asking myself *wadankeygii masaan baa udambaysay?* [What has become of my country?].

During this time, when I was anxious for a positive image of Somalia, a moment of pride presented itself. This moment came during the 1993 summer Olympic games in Barcelona Spain, when the Somali athlete, Abdi Bile took part in the Olympic games' opening ceremony and held up high, for all to see, a sky blue Somali flag with the White star in the middle as he walked alongside other Olympic athletes. Anti-colonial thinker Ngugi Wa Thiong'o (1985) would have said that this moment was merely part of an imperialistic tradition of "flag-waving native rule," (2) about which I am romanticising. But as a child, who witnessed the horrific destruction of his nation, the devastation of his people, and the fragmentation of all he knew, this moment provided me with a powerful social, political, and cultural testimonial of my Somali-ness that up till then, I felt had been amputated from my existence. This moment ruptured the cycle of dehumanizing violence that I witnessed daily on television. It also created an everlasting archival Somali moment that I was able to store in my memory at this impressionable time in my life. I was able to recall and embody this image countless times to escape colonial imagery.

Through this moment, during my formative years, I was able to depart from my colonial existence through acts of psychological travel that bell hooks (1997) called "the fantasy of escape, [with] the promise that what is lost will be found, rediscovered, and returned. For Black folks, reconstruction and archaeology of memory makes return possible" (p.173). Escaping for me meant being able to travel to my beloved *wadan* [country] intact, free from Eurocentric hegemonic discourse, imagery, and historization. Through these journeys I was able to travel to my homeland to see life as I knew it, to be part of a community that was rich with history and culture. These journeys enabled me to experience various aspects of life in my *wadan*. The re-experiencing of the simplest things: taking a drive with my father to school in the morning, walking to the local shops, or going to one of Xamar's national parks, gave me the most joy. Those memories grounded me when I was being uprooted, they provided protection when I was most fragile, and they have helped reclaim my resilient Somali character.

A Cultural Disconnect

Positive cultural conceptualisations, which played such a pivotal role in my identity struggles, is virtually absent in the minds of the 'Say-Walahi' generation. Accordingly, Somali youth always begin articulating their Somali-ness from the darkest moments in our history. This script usually begins from 1991 when the civil war broke out and the country has been in a state of anarchy ever since. This colonial historization is written about Somalia in practically every encyclopaedia, and newspaper article, and is expressed in every media broadcast about Somalia.

Sadly though, Somali youth express this notion at every Somali event and community gathering. Thus, their souls are loaded with dehumanizing Western rhetoric and they are immersed in language that negate their Indigenous culture, language, and histories. The colonial language is the language 'Say-Walahi' generation are conditioned to utilise to express their national Somali aspirations. But language is vital to a soul's sense of power and self-identification. "The bullet was the means of physical subjection. Language [is] the means of ... spiritual subjection" (Wa Thiong'O, 1985, p.9). As such, by speaking and expressing themselves through foreign colonial ideologies the 'Say-Walahi' youth further accept colonization into their Somali identities thus embodying self-inflicted injuries to their wounded Somali national character. What is overtly tragic for the 'Say-Walahi' generation is the fact they cannot recall any lived memories of Somalia prior to the civil war, and they do not possess Afkii Hooyo [mother tongue] to collectively unlock the rich history of their colonial-resistant tradition. According to Wa Thiong'o (1985), the African "resistant tradition is reflected in the patriotic defense of the people's...national culture, [and] their defense of the democratic struggle in all nationalities inhabiting the same territory" (p. 2). Consequently, their ability to draw on the resilient Somali character that Somalis have utilised for generations to engage in the struggles against colonialism is very limited amongst our youth. This Somali national character is made up of an extraordinary desire to be free from all oppression and it is locked both in our genetic and physiological make up as Somalis. Somalis have fought both British and Italian colonial rule, ultimately gaining their independence in 1960 (Adam, 2008). Our national character has enabled us to collectively survive structural displacement, colonial captivity, and the brutality of physical and psychological domination as a people.

I will employ a comparative analysis to demonstrate the cultural disconnect between the *'Say-Walahi'* youth generation and the older generation of Somalis. To conduct my analysis, I will first examine Ayanla Daad's English speech at the first Annual Somali Youth Summit in Columbus Ohio. This summit was a three day conference aimed at highlighting community role models for Somali youth. Ayanla Daad is a young Somali internet blogger, who's been living in the United States for fifteen years. Next, I would like to compare Daad's Speech to Ali Mirre's address at the summit. Ali Mirre is a Somali legend who wrote "Soomaaliyeey toosoo" [Somalia wake up] in 1947. "Soomaaliyeey toosoo" is the national anthem of Somalia sung by generations of school-aged children in Somalia.

I would like to utilise Ngugi Wa Thiong'o's (1985) work on the politics of colonial languages in the African continent to examine the language that Daad made use of to address the audience at the summit. Ayanla Daad's segment of the video presentation begins with him saying "Hi. My name is Ayanla Mohamood Daad. Today my lecture is going to be on Somali politics and how our leaders have been held unaccountable for their action." With this brief introduction, we see a young man who has stepped outside of his own language, culture, and history to express his colonized views about Somalia. As such, Daad does not introduce himself in Somali nor greet the audience with a traditional Somali welcome. In essence, with his first few English words, the cultural disconnect that exists between himself and the greater Somali community that he is addressing is quite evident. Wa Thiong'o' (1985) would argue that language as a means of communication is a product of and is reflective of the "real language of life" elsewhere; it could never be spoken or written properly to reflect the real life of the community (p. 16). Although, the summit took place in the United States and a large majority of the Somali attendees speak English, the mere fact that the young man is speaking about Somalia in English stresses his inability to articulate a Somali voice.

In the next segment of the video, Daad appears wearing a Black suit standing behind a podium at the summit giving his formal speech. He begins by saying "Hello countrymen, distinguished and honorary guests, fellow peers," once again affirming Wa Thiong'o's (1985) contention that a foreign language is unable to express the Indigenous feelings of African people. Although, Daad welcomes the guests, his usage of the English language to deliver his reception inadvertently disconnects him from some of the guests whom he is trying to welcome. Among his audience were the aforementioned Somali icon, Ali Mira, Mahamed Shiikh, a leading Somali publisher and author, and Hussan Ali Mira, the first Somali PhD holder from Princeton University, who, interestingly enough spoke at the summit about the importance of Somali culture and language. In fact, all the above guests spoke about the importance of Somali language, culture, and heritage. Yet there he was, a hopeful youth, through no fault of his own, delivering a speech in English; totally out of line with the nationalistic message that his audience sorely needed.

It is in this state of cultural disconnect that this young man begins to draw on Eurocentric hegemonic discourse, imagery, and historitization to articulate the current State of Affairs in Somalia. As he goes on to state "We are gathered here in large part because of the deep patriotism that we share for our country. At this very moment our nation is facing a peril worse than that of Darfur. The erosion and decimation of basic infrastructure along with human life and mass scale [destructions] never seen before has created thousands of refugees in their own country." According to Wa Thiong'o (1985), "culture does not just reflect the world of images but actually, through those very images, conditions a child to see that world in a certain way, the colonial child was made to see the world and where he stands in it, as seen defined by or reflected in the culture of the language of imposition" (p.17). Consequently, Daad, a youth who has lived most of his life in the United States, who is constantly bombarded with violent images of fleeing refugees, war, and destruction of his homeland, projects what Wa Thing'o (1985) terms "the power of the language of imposition" on African children.

The young man then goes on to mark Somalis geographical landscape by naming major cities and towns in Somalia by stating that "As I stand here today the... rumblings of this contest can be heard from the streets of *Mogadishu, Hargeya, Bossaso, Baydhabo, Kismyoo*, and every other city and village, where the rule of law is to be respected. This is in large part due to the lack of government that our nation has witnessed in the past two decades". To my astonishment, the youth even pronounces the names of Somali cities with an Americanized accent. Daad is a Somali - he physically embodies that identity - and yet here he was speaking like a non-native Somali speaker at this community event. After that, the youth resorts to colonial rhetoric once again by stating that Somalis problems are due to "uneducated men [who] have sought a divisive *Qabiil* [tribal] system' and he thus essentially drops what Wa Thiong'o (1985) calls the cultural time bomb a youthful, largely Somali audience who is present at the summit:

> The biggest weapon wielded and actually daily unleashed against collective defiance is the cultural bomb. The effect of a cultural bomb is to annihilate a people's beliefs in their names, in their language, in their environment, in their heritage of struggle, in their unity, in their capacities and ultimately in themselves. It makes them see their past as one wasteland of non-achievements and it makes them distance themselves from that wasteland. It makes them want to identify with that which is furthest removed from themselves...with all the forces that would stop their own spring of life. (p.3)

Near the end of his speech, Daad begins laying down his vision for a new dawn in Somalia stating "when this day comes, Somalis can rest assure that this great land [Somalia] that stretches from the beautiful mountain top of *Hargesa* to the sea shining city *Mogadishu* will not be ruled by the rules of the jungle, but by a set of common values..." The young man's conceptualisation of his vision of a greater Somalia imbued with such colonial ideology and imagery, as Wa Thiongo' (1985) would argue, is symbolic of the cultural disconnect between the identity that the youth embodies and the ideals that he has internalised. As such, by injecting the word "jungle" into his speech and alluding to the belief that Somalia is a primitive lawless country, he is inadvertently ascribing further injury to the Somali national character which he is patriotically trying to represent.

I'd like to now turn my attention to Ali Mire's presentation to examine how he uses Somali language, oral literature, and Indigenous culture to take some of the Somali youth that were present at the summit on a journey of cultural re-discovery. To conduct my analysis, I would like to utilise Ali Mire's own voice to highlight how he uses

Indigenous Somali culture to produce knowledge to try to reconnect the youth with their history and their Somali identity. Moreover, I would like to employ different anti-colonial ideas to theorise Ali Mire's presentation.

Ali Mire's presentation begins with him singing "*Soomaaliyeey toosoo*" [Somalia wake up] anthem, which he authored in 1947 during Somalia's bloody struggle for independence against British and Italian colonial rule (Ato, 2008). With his singing, Ali Mire, a man now in his eighties, is trying to connect the youth to the land of their ancestors, their histories, and take them on a journey of self-discovery. Moreover, he is speaking to the fragmented identities that the youth embody. As such, "Soomaaliyeey toosoo" takes the youth to a place from which they can begin conceptualising their Somali-ness, free from the dehumanizing discourse and imagery, by speaking of the past. Dei (1999) in his essay, *Rethinking the role of Indigenous knowledges in the Academy,* describes the past as offering "a means of staking out a position as African, which is outside of the identity that has been, and continues to be, constructed by Euro-American ideology (p. 125). It is with this mind-set that Ali Mire sets the course for his presentation as he sings:

> *Soomaaliyeey toosoo*
> *Toosoo isku tiirsada ee*
> *Hadba kiina taagdaranee*
> *Taageera waligiinee*
> *Idinkaa isu tooqaayoo*
> *Idinkaa isu taamaayee*
> *Aadamuhu tacliin barayoo*
> *Waddankiisa taamyeeloo*
> *Sharcigaa isku kiin tolayoo*
> *Luuqadaa tuwaaxid ahoo*
> *Arligiina taaka ahoo*
> *Kuma kala tegeysaan oo*
> *Tiro ari ah oo dhaxalaa*
> *Sideed laydin soo tubayoo*
> *Ninba toban la meel marayoo*
> *Cadowgiin idiin talin oo*
> *Tuldo geel ah oo dhacan baad*
> *Toogasho u badheedhanee*
> *Ma dhulkaas dhanee tegeybaan*
> *Ninna dhagax u tuurayn*

Quaran aan hubkuu tumayo
Tooreyda dhaafayn
Oo aan taar samayn karin
Uur kutaallo weynaa
Hadba waxaan la taahaayoo
Togagga uga qaylshaa
Nin dalkiisii cadow taaboo
U tol waayey baan ahayee
Hadba waxaan laa ooyaayoo
Oo ilmadu iiga qubaneysaa
Iqtiyaar nin loo diidoo
La addoon sadaan ahayee

(Ali Mire, as cited in Ato, 2008)

As Ali Mire sings past the introduction he begins moving his hands and his body to stress the importance of all Somalis to take part in their national struggle against colonialism in an effort to inspire his youthful, mainly English-speaking Somali audience and to communicate the message of the Somali unity. He first appeals to the consciousness of his audience by stating that "*Aadamuhu tacliin barayoo, Waddankiisa taamyeeloo*" [you were the ones educated, support your nation]. After that he goes on to speak to colonial strategies of divide and conquer by singing "*Arligiina taaka ahoo, Kuma kala tegeysaan oo, Tiro ari ah oo dhaxalaa, Sideed laydin soo tubayoo, Ninba toban la meel marayoo, Cadowgiin idiin talin oo*" [you were lined up like sheep to be inherited, in rows, and the enemy will ravage you row by row]. Ali Mire with those words is speaking to the importance of unity in the face of colonial domination, which is a chorus that is repeated throughout the anthem. Additionally, by reciting those words, which he authored more than five decades ago, as a community Elder, he is transmitting vital Indigenous knowledge to the youth. Wane (2008) describes the importance of the role of Elders: "the quality and the quantity of Indigenous knowledge depends on the age and particular role of a person in society. Indigenous knowledges are stored in people's minds and dispersed through stories, songs, proverbs, and everyday practices" (p.192). As such, by delivering his address in person, he not only brings significance to the historical moments that he is speaking of, some of which he has lived through, but he is also producing historical knowledge as he speaks.

Ali Mire recalls some of the bloodiest moments of Somali history as he sings "*Tuldo geel ah oo dhacan baad, Toogasho u badheedhanee,*

57

Ma dhulkaas dhanee tegeybaan, Ninna dhagax u tuurayn" [you have prepared yourself for the struggle, this land cannot be taken, some will throw stones at the colonialists]. At that moment he becomes a monumental figure honouring the struggles of the Somali peoples against colonial rule. Ali Mire's revolutionary words remind me of the five monuments of Hawo Tako, SYL, Dagax Tuurr, Mohammed Abdullah Hassan, and Ahmed Gurey, the ones who stood tall in the heart of *Xamar* [Mogadishu] to honour Somali heroes who fought and died in the struggle for freedom against colonial rule. Like the monuments, Ali Mire is an archetypal figure that signifies a historic journey in Somalia's past. As such, Mire, singing the above words, becomes "a living memory bank [who] act[s] as [a] mirror and as a form of working archive... through the use of oral poetry to formalise memory of the past, and to make the memory of the past comprehensible and accessible (Schenb, 2007, p. 98). More importantly, by revisiting the past and embracing the histories of the Somali identity after the tragic partition of Africa, Ali Mire is speaking of a wholesome culture and of a self–recovery process, which he hopes to initiate with his address.

As Ali Mire's singing of the anthem comes to an end, he hands over the torch to the Somali youth attending the conference, igniting their souls by stating that " *waxan jeclaan lahaa inaan dhalin yarada lakan uga sheego hadallo kooban kuwaasoo aad hore u mashaqasheen oo ah in xoogga qaranku wuxuu kujiraa dhalin yarada. Sidaas darteed, waa inaan isu diyaarino sidii aan wax ugu qaban lahayn wadankeena.* [I would like to mention a few words that you have all have heard before, which are that the strength of the nation is in the youth. Therefore, you all should prepare to serve your country]. Then he begins stressing the importance of Somali culture and language: "*lugagd Somaliadee waaxxy cammed taxhy laqadaha ougo hougabadem"* [Somali language is one of the strongest languages]. At that moment Ali Mire was engaged in a Somali language campaign to promote *Afka Hyoo* [the mother tongue]. In many ways this section of his address speaks to the song *Af qalaad aqoontu miyaa?* [Is foreign language knowledge?] This song was written in the 1960's by Ali Sugula as a part of the resistance movement to oppose the colonial languages in Somalia, and was later sung by Halimo Kalif Magool to promote Somali Language after independence. He proceeds to compare Somali language to English as he states "*Ingsesko marku maal seegoyo yoohoo odanuya here ama there"* [for instance when one wants to point out something in a specific location there are only two words that one can use which are here and there]. *"Afo Somaligona waxy Ladahy halcan, halkar, halqo, halqas"*. The literary translation that Ali Mire provides to draw a comparison between English and Somali is essentially *"Oggoli oo waxbarashadu wey egtehee, af gumeyste ayeynu addoon u nahay"* [Education is not being slaves to the colonial language]. Moreover, he is stating that "Every language is custodian of its speakers' cultural experiences…in a loss of language there is a loss of knowledge and wisdom" (Wane, 2008, p.192). Consequently, his illustration subconsciously ruptures the Eurocentric discourse that the young Daad has externalised. According to Wane (2008), "Eurocentric discourses serve the purpose of justifying the neo-colonial agenda, which remains deeply embedded in…education" (p.192). In essence, with his comparison, Ali Mire is inadvertently saying " *Af qalaad aqoontu miyaa, miyaa miyaa'* (Sugula, 1960) [Is foreign language knowledge? No, no]. More importantly though, Ali Mire's linguistic exercise offers an Indigenous Somali lens, as Dei (1999) would argue, from which the largely young audience can interpret and interrogate colonial discourse. Dei (1999) explains Indigenous knowlegdes as being:

> [T]he epistemic saliency of culture, traditional values, beliefs systems and world views in any Indigenous society that are imparted to the younger generation by community elders. Such knowledge constitutes an Indigenous informed epistemology. It is a worldview that shapes the community's relationships with the surrounding environments. It is the product of the direct experience of nature and its relationship with the social. It is knowledge that is crucial for the survival of society. It is knowledge that is based on cognitive understanding and interpretations of social, physical and spiritual worlds. It includes concepts, beliefs and perceptions, and experiences of the local people and their natural human-built environments. (p.114)

The final section of Ali Mire's address that I am going to be analysing is his *Gabay* [A form of Somali oral tradition] which he recites towards the end of his address. According to Hawa Jibril, the legendary Somali oral traditionalist, *Gabyoo* "were sung, and recited in spoken form, and were passed on by memory across generations, with a strong respect for precision of wording and authorship" (p. 14). Ali Mires' approach is libratory because it transforms the summit from a Eurocentric symposium to a *Geedka Hoostiisa*- the Indigenous Somali communal space- as a result of the *Gabay* that he recites. As such, by utilising Somali tradition, he transforms into becomes a village Elder standing in the middle of the circle beneath the tree, with the artistic ancient language that he uses, and the Somali bodies present at the summit together signifying a *Geedka Hoostiisa* communal meeting. His delivery is quite significant because it places the power of the collective voice in the hands of the community through consensus building and tradition, as he composes the *Gabay*:

> *jeeroo xaaladda taagan,*
> *dadkaygu uu kaxumaado,*
> *oo xoogage kalaqaybsan,*
> *xero isugu keeno,*
> *oon dhulkeyga xoreeyo,*
> *oon xinjir dhiigleh kudaadsho,*
> *oo xabashi aan kakexeeyo,*
> *oo xaqey lay ogolaado,*
> *xumaaneey kuma diido,*
> *xaragooy kuma doono,*
> *xariirey kuma qaato,*
> *xilkas aan noqon maayoo,*
> *xaawo reyseheeda,*
> *xagga intaan kahagoogtiyo,*
> *xishood ba uboodo.*

Ali Mira cited in Ato, 2008

English Translation

> In the current state of affairs
> My country is wronged
> If I bring my divided strengths together
> If my blood is spilled for my nation
> And I expel the Ethiopian forces for my country
> And my rights are restored
> Badness I don't refuse you
> Bride I don't seek you
> Silk I don't wear you
> I will not be irresponsible

Ali Mire essentially ruptures the colonial social construction of the Somali identity that the *'Say-Walahi'* generations have internalised and he takes some of the willing youth with him on a journey through

60

his *Gabay* back to their origins. Accordingly, Ali Mire provides a liberating Somali Indigenous narrative that is rooted in Somali history, culture, and ancient traditions. It is through his *Gabay* that he plants the seeds of tomorrow and initiates a decolonizing journey for the Somalis at the conference. Dei (1999) would argue that Ali Mire's address was " a necessary journey in which he reclaim[ed] aspects of his culture and tradition that can be narrated as a whole and as [a] fundamental human [need]...to affirm and to resist an amputation of [his] past, history and culture"(p.125).

I would like to now utilise Molefi Asante's works on Afrocentricity in Education to examine the decolonizing process that one youth undergoes during the youth Summit. My aim is to show how Ali Mire's oral presentation has enabled this young man to re-claim elements of his Somali-ness. I would like to pay particular attention to how the youth first begins by speaking English as he is sitting on the closing panel with other Somali youth on the last day of the summit and then how he begins utilising *Afka Somaliga* as he talks about *Suugaan* [Somali songs, dances, *Gabay*, etc.].

The youth whom I am focused on is an unnamed nineteen year old Somali teen. What is remarkable about this youth is the fact that he attended the second day of the summit wearing a *macwees* [traditional Somali men's bottom wear] and a *cimaamad* [Somali men's headwear], and he spoke about the importance of Somali youth holding on to their Somali culture. Ironically though, his presentation was in English. However, on the third day, as I stated earlier, the youth is inspired to speak Somali as he begins to speak about Somali *Suugan*.

The youth starts his closing statements by saying:

> The first day was interesting, because it was the first time ever. It was nice to see other speakers from North Carolina and stuff like that. And mostly I was impressed by the guy who wrote the Somalia *toos toos* anthem, and I had an opportunity to meet a Somali legend that I normally would not have if I didn't come to the event. So that was pretty much the highlight of the day that I felt was the most important, the most necessary.

The above statement indicates that the youth is impressed with the fact that he met the Somali icon, and that he was being grounded in his own history and culture. Asante (1991) would argue that the young man is no longer feeling alien and/or like an outsider because he met a Somali hero who looks like him; moreover, the youth is being grounded in Afrocentricity. Accordingly, Afrocentricity "is a frame of reference wherein phenomena are viewed from the perspective of the African person. This approach seeks in every situation the appropriate centrality of the African person" (Asante, 1991.p.171). This is a valuable lesson for a Somali youth who is constantly exposed to Eurocentric discourse, and dehumanizing imagery about his homeland and culture.

The youth then goes on to talk about the second day of the summit and he, in effect, begins to see himself outside the civil war regime and the violent images that are imposed on his Somali-ness, as he states:

> But [I] got to meet the [man] who does the Somali publishing from Canada & Sweden and looking at his dedication and the time and effort that he put into collecting all these different Somali books that were written so long time ago that were unfortunately lost during the civil war...It shows that Somalia was known before the civil war...that the whole world did not just get an image of us through the war

This statement shows that as a result of the youth seeing a Somali publisher who has worked tirelessly to collect and preserve Somali text, he discovers that he has a past to be explored and treasured. Although, the youth continues to be immersed in civil war rationalisations, his perspective is quite different from Ayanla Daad's perception of his Somali identity, which I analysed earlier, due to the fact that he met a Somali publisher. In essence, it is because of this meeting that the youth "is shown how to see with new eyes and hear with new ears" (Asante, 1991, p.174) on issues pertaining to his Somali culture and history. As a result, the young man is now able to begin imagining his nation free from war, anarchy, and destruction because of the books that he saw at the summit.

In the final segment of the closing panel the youth is shown speaking Somali, stating that, *"Cearaha Somaliad ennan kaso qaueb jalo wane chaclahy, Chandare euo Dantoo...Somali hesso wanchacalah, hadan waqatry heelo wahane waedya hoyadey, uio abahy, uioo ayahday. Ayadey wahxan waydea ayaoyo eeshaje hel Gabayuio mahmah"* [I love dancing to Somali traditional dances the *Chandare* and the *Dantoo*...I like Somali songs. If I have a chance I ask my parents or my grandmother to recite me a Somali *Gabay* for me]. The fact that the youth begins expressing himself in Somali indicates that he not only sees Ali Mire as "a Somali legend" as he put it, but that the youth has immersed himself in Ali Mire's message of holding on to Somali language and culture. Consequently, the youth has taken up the Somali language as a medium of self-expression.

In addition, his use of the Somali language signifies that the youth has undergone a cultural re-claiming process that grounds the youth in his Somali-ness as a result of attending the summit. Accordingly, the youth was conscious of his Somali language and culture. But the mere fact that he was utilising English to express himself spoke to the fact that he was not completely grounded in his Somali Indigenous culture. Malidoma Some's novel *Of Water and the Spirit* eloquently captures his own cultural initiation journey. In his book, Malidoma Somé shows his internal struggles to free himself from the colonial education which he received at missionary school. Malidoma Some questions the legitimacy of colonialism in the missionary institution that has fashioned his soul, and he eventually ends up leaving. Even though, he physically finds his way back to his village, he is culturally dislocated and never manages to ground his soul in his Indigenous Dagara ways of living and knowing until he is put through a rigorous initiation process. Similar to Malidoma Some's journey, this Somali youth, who has spent most of his life living in the United States, comes to eject Eurocentric conceptualisation of his Somali-ness from his psyche and finds his way to the Somali community through the summit. Yet the youth is unable to completely break free from Eurocentric ideology and ways of knowing until he hears Ali Mire, a Somali Elder, and his likes at the summit. It is only then that the youth is able to decolonize his soul. In Malidoma Some's novel, community Elders view Malidoma's initiation process as finding the centre

> Each one of us possesses a center that he had grown away from after birth...The center is both within and without. It is everywhere. But we must realize that it exists, find it and be with it, for without the center we cannot tell who we are, where we come from, and where we are going (Malidoma Some, 1994, p.198).

The youth's centre is highlighted by his ability to draw reference to Somali Indigenous dances *Chandare* and *Dantoo* and Somali oral traditions *Gabay* and *Mahamah* in *Afe Somali*. As such, the youth is no longer looking outside himself to express his identity in a foreign language and he is now utilising Somali *dahqan* from a Somali Indigenous perspective.

Conclusion

In reflecting back at my own story of resistance to colonial imagery and conceptualisation of Somalia as a famine-stricken nation that is engulfed in a bloody war, I was able to reflect on the importance of having a positive Somali narrative to draw on as a means of survival. Revisiting some of my lived experiences as a Somali who witnessed a colonial script get ascribed to my beloved homeland, I was able to comprehend my endurance mechanisms. Then having an opportunity to critically analyse the Somali youth summit in Ohio with an anti-colonial lens and looking at the cultural disconnect that subsists between the *'Say-Walahi'* generation and the generation of Elders that have fought for Somalia's independence, I was able to grasp the importance of Somali *dhaqan* to our survival as a people. Having undertaken this journey, I find myself in a peculiar place. On one hand, I have witnessed Somali cultural knowledge gaps between generations of Somalis. On the other hand, I am better able to understand and appreciate the countless sacrifices our forbearers have made for us. I have also come to the realisation that every generation of Somalis will embody their struggle differently and that we all carry something in us that is uniquely Somali. It is important for every generation to unlock elements of their Somali-ness and engage in their own struggle. In agreement with Franz Fanon (1967) "Every generation must come out of its relative obscurity to discover its' mission and either betray it or fulfil it" (126). The consequences of not taking up the fight will be detrimental and costly for future generations of Somali.

Chapter 6
Conclusion

Now that I have narrated some of my untold stories, where do I go from here? How do I re-claim my Somali-ness from the margins? Where is my path to salvation? How do I reconnect to my ancestral way of life? How do I hear my own Indigenous voice and make sense of it as I live in a distant land? In this chapter, I will first reflect on my own research journey. Second, I discuss future directives for research on the *'Say-Walahi'* generation. Finally, I will take a few moments to collect my breath and think about the lessons that I have learned from taking this journey.

What has my journey been like? When I first started writing my proposal for this book I was guided by my inner voice that wanted to speak about being Somali in the Canadian landscape. This internal voice drew me into conversations with myself about my own identity struggles and issues of self-survival. With my own voice, I was confident that I could tell some of my own stories, theorise some of my lived experiences, and reflect on my journey of coming to a place of healing; yet after having taken this journey, many questions remain unanswered. This journey has been full of frustration and anxiety, as I have told the stories of how I learned to overcome colonization by holding onto my Somali identity, culture and language. This process also includes how my journey diverges and converges with the journeys' of other Somali youth in the diaspora.

I've come to realise that I am now closer to speaking about my Somali-ness with a complete self, however, I am not yet grounded enough in my Indigenous *dahaqn* to speak in the voices of my ancestors. As I wrote this book, I felt incomplete and I kept asking myself "Where is my Somali-ness?" I felt extremely ill-equipped to conduct this research at times. This question overshadowed my research as I struggled to write. One of the most difficult aspects of this journey was the fact that it was rooted in my previous homeland which I left as a child. Though I had grown up Somali, my home environment was Somali, and my soul is Somali; I, nevertheless, found it very difficult to find my way back home and speak with an Indigenous Somali voice. I had never questioned myself prior to undertaking this journey because I was so sure of myself. Even as a displaced person who has spent most of his life living in exile, I know that I belong to a culture and a community with a rich history because my life revolved around the Somali community in Toronto. Still, I felt something of significance was missing. As I conducted my research, I had to pause in order to re-trace my own background because I realised that my soul was fragmented and out of place. It was then that I decided to rely on my memories to convey my stories with an authentic respect for my youthful understanding of the events that unfolded around me. These stories made it easier for me to speak about a missing part of my Somali-ness that I needed to honour and reclaim.

My stories are real and I never thought the day would come when I would finally get an opportunity to tell them. My memory bank was filled with raw experiences of being marked as a Somali in the White Canadian nation space. I vividly recollect my first instances of becoming aware of the colonial gaze upon me and my people, and the terror of being read through it. How could I ever forget sitting in an all-White classroom and listening to a student conduct a presentation about how honourable the 'Canadian peace machines' were in Bosnia and Somalia, knowing full well that the latter nation is where the 'Somalia affair' scandal erupted throughout world news? My memories are personal yet they speak to a national identity struggle of the Somali people, because they speak to injustices that have been inflicted upon us. In speaking about them I, therefore, must honour Somali *dhaqan* and traditional *Xeer* [customs]. On the other hand, because there were not many models in the academy that offered Indigenous Somali epistemology and ontology, I also had to trust myself and follow my own path to complete this journey.

In the midst of frustration, anxiety, and a desire to speak with a resilient Somali voice, I decided to own the journey and ground the process in my Somali-ness, while conforming to the academy. This decision made it easier for me to collect my inner most private thoughts about my Somali self. As such, I let my consciousness speak through my research journey and as a result I was able to find interconnectedness between my current self and my past. With this mind-set, I was able to leave the Eurocentric ways of examining knowledge. This was not an easy task at all, and I was forced to search hard and deep into my soul to narrate some of my embodied Indigenous knowledges; consequently it was only then that I began to feel like I was beginning to hear my soul speak. The embodiment of my Somali-ness became the Indigenous praxis of my research. I had wanted to do this research for a long time and wanted to engage in this journey to become whole again. My journey was bittersweet and yet unimaginably fulfilling, because it forced me to dig deeply into my roots. This journey has taken me back to the lands of my forefathers in Somalia where the *dhaqan badyio* is still thriving. As such, by studying Somali *dhaqan* in my own life, I was able to bring forth a suppressed cultural consciousness which finally lead me to "the awareness of the existing knowledge in my blood and bones" (Wane, 2006, p. 102). It was only then that I was truly able to articulate my thoughts through an Indigenous Somali lens and learn how to bring elements of '*dhaqan badyio*' into the forefront.

Dahaqn badiyo is essentially the camel-herding lifestyle of the communal existence of my forefathers who were *reer badiyo* [people of the Badiyo]. This Indigenous way of life has been a part of my ancestral heritage for centuries. This way of life encompasses a holistic Somali culture by embodying tradition, community, and an intergenerational connectedness; it is a way of life that also speaks to the journeys which we have travelled as a people. *Reer badiyo* peoples are camel herding communities and they often resettle with their entire communities in search of water and a greener ecology suitable for their livestock. They also relocate with livestock when infectious insects infest their environment and/or when there are *colaad* [tensions with other communities]. What is most remarkable about these communities is that they load and travel with their *Aqal* Somali on their camels everywhere.

Aqal Somali is a hut style house that *reer badiyo* communities live. The literary English translation of *Aqal* Somali is Somali house. *Aqal* Somali is typically made of a "semicircular support and a middle pillar (*udub-dhebaas*). The semicircular supports (*dhigo*) are made from light wood from the branches and roots of certain trees; the conversing...consists of woven mats; for additional impermeability a tarpaulin is draped on the top" (Abdullahi, 2001, p.105). The sequence captured in Figure 6-1 show a typical *Reer badiyo* community.

Figure 1. Aqal Somali in Reer Badiyo community (Geocities, 2008).

Before relocating these communities, the first step involves sending a *sham* on a journey to inspect a suitable location to move the community. The *saham* is typically a knowledgeable person in the community and trained in the techniques of *saham doon* [the relocation journey]. The sham's relocation tasks include finding a suitable environment for community with water supplies, optimal ecological environment, and free of hostile communities which would be competing for the natural resources of *badiyo*. The following picture captured in Figure 6-2 shows Aqaloo Soomali on a caravan of camels typically after the *sham* has indicated a new location to resettle.

As a member of the Somali community residing in Toronto, Canada, I can say that we have travelled across the globe to settle in this land. Most of us have experienced a *sham* process of some sort as individuals, family members, and as a community. Our collective resettlement experiences have not been easy.

As a displaced Somali who has resettled and re-established his roots in Canada, I offer the *'Say-Walahi'* age group and future generations of Somali Canadians the concept of travelling the treacherous journey back towards their Somali self and the recovery of their Somali voice, with their *Aqal* Somali. As such, by journeying through critical, Somali-affirming, life-lessons, by rediscovering their Indigenous knowledges and their communities, they will never be displaced and/or dislocated. More importantly, this process will allow the *'Say-Walahi'* generation to recognise and resist all the ways in which misrepresentation has framed them, because it will allow them to see themselves outside the Eurocentric discourse and imagery that is ascribed to their identity. This process will also allow them to embrace their past and make sense of the social realities that dislocate them in every aspect of their lives. The sceptics might raise questions as to whether the *Aqal* Somali concept has any relevance in the lives of the *'Say-Walahi'* generation living in Canada. My lived realities, which have been documented in this research, demonstrate that it is crucial to the survival of Somali-Canadian youth to take up elements of Somali *dhaqan*. In addition, this concept is adaptable to any environment and can be easily implemented in Canada.

Figure 2. Aqal **Somali on a caravan (Geocities, 2009).**

My future research will build on my previous research and interest in continuing to study identity issues of the *'Say-Walahi'* generation. I am interested in making the connection of various elements of Somali *dhaqan* including: *Geedka Hoostiisa*i, the Somali oral tradition of *Gabay*, and *dhaqan badiyo* as way of accounting for the lived experiences of Somali youth and as an instrument for voice recovery. I anticipate this study will assist us in conceptualising and theorising the lived experiences of Somali-Canadian youth both from a historical and a contemporary perspective. Consequently, this study will inevitably initiate a better understanding of the complex issues Somali youth face in Canadian society in their own voices. I am deeply motivated to create a body of scholarly literature that will be utilised by future generations of Somali Canadians to make sense of their Somali cultural knowledges in Canada. My interests extend beyond the academy, as I am concerned with community's well-being and collective action to achieve community interests. Therefore, I will carry out action oriented research that will provide long term community solutions for the issues of the *'Say-Walahi'* generation that are grounded in Somali *dhaqan*. The following are five research questions I will look at:

- How do Somali-Canadian youths see Somali culture in Canadian society?
- How many identities do they embody? How do they negotiate those identities? What are some tensions that arise from the identities that they embody?
- How do the *'Say-Walahi'* generation deal with stereotypes about themselves and their culture?
- How does the *'Say-Walahi'* generation see mainstream society; members of the Somali community; and other non-Somali youths?
- What is the schooling experience like for Somali-Canadian youth?

Although this journey has been long and unpredictable, I've taken a challenging path to arrive at this point. Through many trials and tribulations, I held onto various elements of Somali *dhaqan* as I manoeuvred through the Canadian landscape. I've been presented with a unique opportunity to reflect on some of the events that have taken place in my life in this research process. As a result I have a better sense of who I am and how far I've come, and I now believe that I've finally made significant strides in my quest to reach a spiritual place where I can enrich my greater purpose in life. This research has allowed me to engage in work that enhanced my understanding of the role that Somali culture has played in my life; conversely, I understand that Somali culture might not be as instrumental in other Somalis' lives. In fact, I wish to emphasise that this is not a totalizing outlook, but rather it should be viewed as my perspective. Some might even question the relevance of Indigenous Somali culture in Canada. In response to this sentiment I say, why not embrace the culture that Somali peoples have been utilising to survive for centuries? Embrace your *dhaqan*, compose and recited *Gabay* with sincerity, send forth your inner *saham* bravely, keeping alert to false and disheartening depictions of your reality, and then, when the time and place present themselves, pick up your *Aqal* proudly and move on.

References

Abdullahi, M. D. (2000). *Culture and customs of Somalia.* Westport, CT: Greenwood Publishing Group.

Achebe, C. (1996). *Things fall apart.* London: Heinemann Educational Books.

Adam, M. H. (2008). *From tyranny to anarchy: The Somalia experience.* Trenton, NJ: Red Sea Press.

Aqal Somali —Somalia [Online Image]. (Geocities, 2009). Retrieved October 15, 2008, from Geocities.com. Somali.com. http://www.geocities.com/saidsuleimanabdi/index.htm.

Aqal Somali on a Caravan [Online Image]. (Geocities, 2009). Retrieved January 20, 2009 from Geocitices.com. http://www.geocities.com/saidsuleimanabdi/index.htm.

Asante, K. M. (1991). The Afrocentric idea in education. *Journal of Negro Education, 60(*2), 170-180.

Asante, K. M. (1998). *The Afrocentric idea.* Philadelphia: Temple University Press.

Asante, K. M. (2005). Afrocentricity: Noted on disciplinary positions. In J. Conyers (Ed.), *Afrocentric traditions* (pp. 1-14). New Brunswick, NJ: Library of Congress.

Asante, K. M. (2003). Erasing Racism: The Survival of the American Nation. New York : Prometheus Books.

Ato, A. (Exective Producer) (2008). *Somali youth Summit* Television broadcast].Columbus: Bartamaha. Retrieved February 13, 2008 from www.Bartamaha.com.

Barbes, V.L.& Boddy, J.(1995). *Aman: The Story of a Somali Girl.* New York, NY: Vantage Books.

Bashire, A.(1977). *Haybad waxahn qulanahy dolqana hoyoo,* [We have pride in the land of our mother]. Mogadishu: Wabary Studio.

Capp, J. C.,& Jorgensen, C. (1997). *Traditional Knowledge: Don't leave home without it.* Paper presented at the 62nd North American Wildlife and Natural Resources Conference, Washington, DC.

Christmas, R. (Producer). (1993). *A Place Called Dixon* [Television series]..Toronto: CBC..

Cochrane, T. (1991). Life is a Highway. On Mad Mad World [CD]. New York: Capitol Records.

Dei, G. J. S. (1996). Theoretical Approaches to Study of Race. In G. J. S. Dei (Ed.). *Antiracism Education in Theory and Practice* (pp. 25-46).. Halifax: Frenwood.

Dei, G. J. S., Mszzuca, J., McIssac, E., & Zine, J. (1997) *Reconstructing Drop-Out: A Critical Ethnography of the Dynamics of Black Students' Disengagement from School.* Toronto: University of Toronto Press.

Dei, G. J. S., Hall, B., & Rosenberg (Eds.). (1999) *Indigenous Knowledges in Global Context: Multiple Readings of Our World.* Toronto: University of Toronto Press.

Dei, G. J. S., & Johal, G. S. (Eds.).(2005). Critical Issues in Anti-racist Research Methodologies. New York: Peter Lang.

Dei,G. J. S. (2006). Mapping the Terrain-Towards a New Politics of Resistance. In Dei, G& A Kemp (Ed.), *Anti-Colonialism and Education: The Politics of Resistance,* (pp.1-24). Rotterdam: Sense Publishers.

Dei, G. J. S. (2007). Speaking Race: Silence, Salience, and the Politics of Anti-Racist Scholarship. In Sean P. Hier and B. Singh Bolaria (Ed.) Race *and Racism in the 21st –Century Canada, Continuity, Complexity, and Change,* (pp.53-66). Peterborough, Ontario: Broadview Press.

Dei, G. J. S. (2008). Schooling as Community: Race, Schooling and the Education of African Youth. *Journal of Black Studies, 38* (3), 346-366.

Fanon, F. (2004). *The Wretched of the Earth.* New York, NY: Grove Weidenfeld.

Galabuzi, G. E. (2006). *Canada's Economic Apartheid: The Social Exclusion of Racialized Groups in the New Century.* Toronto, Canada: Canadian Scholar Press.

Graveline, F. J. (1998). *Circle Works: Transforming Eurocentric Consciousness.* Halifax, Canada: Fernwood Publishing.

Hall, S. (1981). The Whites of their Eyes: Racist Ideologies and the Media. In G. Dines and J. Humez (Ed.). *Gender, race and classin media* (pp.1-23). London. Saga Publications.

Hall, S. (1990). Culture Identity and Diaspora Entity: Community, Culture, Difference. In J. Rutherford (Ed.), *Identity* (pp. 222-237). London: Lawrence & Wishart.

Hall, S. (1997). Introduction & The Work of Representation. In S. Hall (Ed.), *Representation: Culture Representation and Signifying*

Practices (pp 1-75). London: Sage Publications.

hooks, b. (1997). Representing Whiteness in the Black Imagination. In Ruth Frankenberg (Ed.), *Displacing Whiteness* (pp. 165-179). Durham, NC: Duke University Press.

Huntington, P, S. (1993). The Clash of Civilizations. *Council of Foreign Affairs*,73 (3)17-45.

Ibrahim, A. (2008). The New Flaneur: Subaltern Cultural Studies, African Youth in Canada and the Semiology of In-Betweenness. *Cultural Studies*, 22(2),, 234-253.

Jabril, H. (2008). *And Then She Said: The Poetry and Times of Hawa Jiril.* Toronto: Jumblies Press.

Laurence, M. (1963). *The Prophet's Camel Bell.* Toronto: McClelland and Stewart Limited

Li, P. (2003). Deconstructing Canada Discourse of Immigration Integration. *Journal of International Migration and Integration.* 4(3), 315-333.

McClintock, A. (1995). The Lady of the Land: Genealogies of Imperialism. In *Imperial Leather. Race, Gender & Sexuality in the Colonial Contest*, (pp.21-37) New York: Routledge.

OHCR. (1967). United Nations Convention Relating to the Status of Refugees. New York.

Richburg, K. (1992, October 15). Western Media Overkill Helps and Harms Somalia Relief Effort. The Toronto Star, pp..A.21.

Schennb,H. (2007). The Oral Artist's Script. In Olaniyan, T., & Quayson, A. (Eds.), *African Literature: Anthology of Criticism and Theory*,(pp.97-100). Toronto: Blackwell Publishing.

Shelton, A. A. (2000). Displaying Cultures & Museum Ethnography and Imperial Science. In E. Hallam & B. Street (Eds.), *Cultural Encounters: Representing 'Otherness'*(pp.155-193). London: Routledge.

Some, M. (1994). *Of Water and the Sprit: Ritual Magic and Imitation in the Life of an African Shaman.* New York, NY: Penguin.

Sugula, A. (1961). *Af qalaad aqoontu miyaa* [Is foreign language knowledge]. Mogadishu: Wabarye Studio.

Stoffman, D. (1995, August). Dispatch from Dixon: More than 4,000 Somali refugees are crowded into Six high-rise condominiums on Dixon Road. Toronto Life, 40, 40-55.

Tator, C., & Henry, F. (2006). The Colour of Democracy Racism in Canadian Soceity (3rd ed.). Toronto: Thomson Nelson.

Wa Thiongo, N. (1985). *Decolonizing the Mind: The Politics of Language in African Literature.* New Hampshire: Heinemann Educational books.

Wane, N. N.(2005). Claming, Writing, Storing and Sharing the Discourse. *Journal of Though, 40* (22), 27- 46.

Wane, N. N. (2006). Is Decolonization possible? In Dei, G. & Kemp A. (Ed.), *Ant-Colonialism and Education: The Politics of Resistance* (87-106). Rotterdam: Sense Publishers.

Wane, N. N. (2008). Mapping the Field of Indigenous Knowledges in Anti-Colonial discourse: A Transformative Journey in Education. *Journal of Race Ethnicity and Education,* 11(2), 183-197.

www.ingramcontent.com/pod-product-compliance
Lightning Source LLC
Chambersburg PA
CBHW031455270326
41930CB00007B/1019